CONCILIUM

concilium 1995/4

THE FAMILY

Edited by
Lisa Sowle Cahill and
Dietmar Mieth

SCM Press · London
Orbis Books · Maryknoll

Published by SCM Press Ltd, 26–30 Tottenham Road, London N1
and by Orbis Books, Maryknoll, NY 10545

Copyright © 1995 Stichting Concilium
English translations © 1995 SCM Press Ltd and Orbis Books, Maryknoll

All rights reserved. No part of this publication may be reproduced, stored in a retrieval system, or transmitted, in any form or by any means, electronic, mechanical, photocopying, recording or otherwise, without the prior written permission of Stichting Concilium, Prins Bernhardstraat 2, 6521 A B Nijmegen, The Netherlands

ISBN: 0 334 03033 1 (UK)
ISBN: 0 88344 885 8 (USA)

Typeset at The Spartan Press Ltd, Lymington, Hants
Printed by Mackays of Chatham, Kent

Concilium Published February, April, June, August, October, December.

Contents

Editorial
    Lisa Sowle Cahill and Dietmar Mieth   vii

The New Testament and the Family
    Carolyn Osiek   1

The History of the Family
    Charles J. Reid, Jr   10

Forms of Cohabitation and Procreation outside Marriage
    Rinus Houdijk   18

The Psychology of Family Relationships
    Sidney Callahan   26

Change in the Family and the Challenges of Contemporary Culture
    Giorgio Campanini   37

Faith, Feminism and the Family
    Linda Woodhead   43

The Family in the 'Peripheral World'
    Enrique Dussel   53

The Family and Moral Decisions: How Should the Christian Family Respond to the New Moral Challenges of Today?
    Marifé Ramos González   66

The Family in the Teaching of the Magisterium
    Norbert Mette   74

The Christian Family as Domestic Church at Vatican II
    Michael A. Fahey   85

The Church as Family in Africa
    F. Kabasele Lumbala   93

Building a Spirituality of Family Life
  MARCIO FABRI DOS ANJOS   99
Family Values and Ideals
  MARCIANO VIDAL   110

Contributors   120

Editorial

The Family

In most of the world's cultures, 'the family' institutionalizes intergenerational biological relationships, expanded and perpetuated by means of marriages between kinship groups. A primary function of families is to channel the procreative potential of sexuality in a socially constructive way, so that the next generation is produced and socialized with stable structures. Traditional institutions of family have been patriarchal and hierarchical in virtually all the world's cultures. Families are also productive and economic units, securing the transmission of property within and among kinship groups. In many societies, family membership establishes the political and religious status of individuals.

In modern industrial societies, the family has often been narrowed to the 'nuclear' family: a married couple with children whose roles and social function reflect a public-private split between work and home. Women's place is in the domestic sphere, where children are nurtured. Men belong in the public sphere of politics and employment, re-entering the home for the emotional support and personal ties largely absent in competitive and economically-driven relationships outside the family. One important challenge to the nuclear family so defined comes from the changing roles of women, and, more slowly, of men, as women assume paid employment outside the home, and men take over more responsibilities within it. The successful care of children is jeopardized; however, all employed adults are expected to devote themselves to their jobs on the traditional model of a husband with a wife at home. This is especially true to the extent that parents lack the support system of the extended family in raising children and meeting other social and economic needs. Especially in view of the rise (and now possibly demise) of the nuclear family model, how can we recognize the moral and social importance of the bonds between parents and children, of the fact that even persons without spouses or children are members of families, and that the responsibilities of adults to their own elders are important along with their responsibilities to their children?

Divorce and single-parent families are now common in the industrialized nations. Women feel less obliged to enter or remain in marriages for financial and social security. Cultural tendencies to value individual freedom and fulfillment over duties to one's mate and children encourage some men, who in past generations might have supported a mistress as well as the marital household, to avoid or terminate marriages with the mothers of their children. Yet, although divorce or abandonment ends a marriage or sexual relationship, it does not end parenthood, and remarriage often extends and reshapes an existing family structure. Moreover, as single parents struggle to balance family and work, and as adults bond together in non-marital units to raise children, questions emerge about the importance of the permanent heterosexual union as the basis for forming a family. An even more radical question is whether inter-generational, biological kinship is still essential to our understanding of what a family is.

New family forms are demanding a renewed or new Christian understanding of family. A theological perspective on these questions is essential to this number of *Concilium*. What impact does the gospel message have on the family: Do the Bible and Christian tradition advance a particular form or forms of the family? What have traditional images of God and of the human condition contributed to our approach to the family today? How has church teaching on the family adapted after Vatican II? How does the practical experience of families challenge some past understanding of family, and contribute to the development of new ones? What resources does Christianity provide for a reconsideration of the roles of family members, for a critique of unjust relationships, and for a spirituality or theology of the family?

Christianity arose within first-century cultures – Jewish, Greek, and Roman – in which male elders exerted tremendous authority over the household, and over the extended family and its property. Women were closely guarded, married off at a young age, and frequently kept secluded within the home (C. Osiek). In Greco-Roman culture, the family and procreation within the family functioned as a means of control by the state, for which citizens were expected dutifully to produce children. Christianity in part challenged the patriarchal family by loosening the bonds of family and religious identity, by modifying men's authority over women, and by proposing permanent virginity as an alternative to marriage. However, the Christian religious sanctification of marriage (as in Ephesians 5) could be dangerous in so far as the patterns of marital subordination in the surrounding culture were incorporated under the aegis of a new exhortation to mutual love (Osiek).

By the fifth century CE, and under the influence of the 'barbarian' Germanic peoples, Jerome and Augustine looked with suspicion on both Roman and pagan practice, and endorsed sexual asceticism. They did not deny, however, that marriage had goods to recommend it. In the eleventh century, papal reforms advanced marriage as a positive alternative to virginity, made free choice of one's marriage partner the norm, and more firmly associated indissolubility with a marriage freely begun. The church, backed up by public authority, also established a canonical judicial system to oversee the marital conduct of Christians in Western Europe (C. Reid). This had an enormous impact on the family, in so far as divorce and remarriage for economic and political motives (including the manipulation of children and women by adult men) became increasingly difficult for families to arrange. But the legacy for the Christian family today is ambiguous. The canonical requirement of consent helped to guarantee personal freedom and equality in the undertaking of marriage and the establishment of a new family. But indissolubility – as well as other legal and moral requirements surrounding sexuality and parenthood – were in practice enacted in the form of laws and external demands rather than presented as attractive ideals for family life (M. Ramos Gonzalez).

Several of our authors trace the development of modern church teaching on the family as it has struggled with this mixed heritage, noting its liabilities, and offering prospects for the future. Many of these centre upon the viability of the image of the 'domestic church' as a means of revitalizing the Catholic family and its relation to the ecclesial community (N. Mette, M. Fahey, F. Kabasele Lumbala). This image, whose reintroduction at the time of the Second Vatican Council Michael Fahey recounts in detail, has special power in societies, as in Africa, where all human relationships are organized around the family, or in ways analogous to family ties (Kabasele Lumbala). In Africa, the church itself is more frequently spoken of as a family than as a people. While the idea that the family is a domestic church may be used pastorally to affirm the important contribution of families to the church, it must also be asked critically whether the hierarchical and even sexist traditions of church organization stand in the way of an effective ministry to the family *as* 'church'. Intercultural dialogue will immeasurably enrich the further Catholic appropriation of this model of family life.

The experiences of Christians in Latin America, in Asia, and in Africa, as well as in North America and Europe, provide a variety of cultural histories and challenges to inform our understanding of the family. For instance, sixteenth-century conquest, colonialism and Christianization had a great impact on families of the so-called 'Third World', or 'World on the Periphery'. Colonization resulted not only in patriarchy, but in racial and cultural domination, and these have affected the experience of families in many cultures (E. Dussel). The possibly more egalitarian but isolated and increasingly fragmented modern nuclear family may be able to learn from traditional co-operative and communitarian models of family. On the other side, older patriarchal forms of marriage and kinship will be modified by the growing expectation of equality in the contemporary family, and by the new importance attributed to marital affection and intimacy, not only in modern cultures, but in official Catholic teaching.

Special challenges for a Roman Catholic theology, spirituality, and morality of family life are the equality of the sexes, the reinvigoration and even the 're-invention' of the meanings of parenthood and of permanent monogamous commitment, both in personal terms and as social institutions (R. Houdijk, M. Fabri dos Anjos, G. Campanini). Past issues of *Concilium* have demonstrated that patriarchal family systems as endorsed by Christian theology and practice have led to violence against women, and inhumane constraint of roles for both sexes. (See, for example, 1989/6, *Motherhood: Experience, Institution, Theology*; 1991/6, *The Special Nature of Women*; 1994/1, *Violence Against Women*; edited by Anne Carr, Elisabeth Schüssler Fiorenza and Mary Shawn Copeland). The question of women's place in the family arises many times in the current issue. Linda Woodhead, writing from an explicitly feminist perspective, affirms the body as a point of rapprochement between feminist and Christian understandings of the family. She argues that the bodily 'blood tie' (extended to the 'one flesh' unity of marriage) is an important, unique, and basic form of relatedness. It can provide a firm foundation for family love, though it must be kept in mind that Christianity resists 'family worship' and the narrowing of ties to exclusive family bonds. Marriage and family have traditionally been axes not only of sexism, but of racism and classism as well. Consequently, not only gender equality, but also social solidarity with those outside one's family, class, ethnic, racial or national group must be part of the socialization which the renewed Christian family provides (S. Callahan, Dussel, dos Anjos, M. Vidal).

Lisa Sowle Cahill
Dietmar Mieth

The New Testament and the Family
Carolyn Osiek

If we could engage in discussion about the family with a group of first-century Christians, we would find that there would be a number of communication gaps. When modern inhabitants of technological societies think of 'family', we think first of all of the nuclear family: father, mother and dependent children. Our first-century people, however – and still members of most cultures today – would think of 'family' rather as the entire network of people related to each other by blood, marriage and other intimate social ties, such as clientage. A second meaning would be the family in its vertical extension, its ancestry. A third, narrower meaning would be all who live under the same roof of an extended household: nuclear family, other relatives, slaves, renters, etc. While the nuclear family certainly existed, neither the Hebrew word *bayit*, nor the Greek *oikos* or *oikia*, nor the Latin *domus* or *familia* bear that meaning. In fact, none of these ancient languages had a word that meant primarily the nuclear family.

The pages that follow will sketch in broad lines the contours of the family as it was known by Jews, Greeks and Romans in the Mediterranean world of the first Christian centuries. No attempt can be made here to draw fine distinctions among the different cultural and legal systems. From the perspective of twenty centuries, those distinctions are not nearly as significant as the ways in which the overall picture differs from that of our day.

The family system, like the political system, was patriarchal. The legal authority of male elders extended over everyone in their household and in their extended family, including adult children, as well as over the property of all these persons. In practice, however, adult males, even women and slaves to a certain extent, controlled their own property. Women owned and inherited property in their own right, but technically required the permission of a male guardian to administer it – the Roman law of *tutela*. In the New Testament period, however, exceptions to this rule seem to have been more prevalent than the strict observance of it. Augustan legislation, for example, under the need to encourage population increase, granted exemption from the law to freeborn women who produced three children and to freedwomen who produced four, an indication of how lightly *tutela* was regarded.

The moral authority of mothers, though not embedded in civil law, was just as binding. The modern assumption that the fourth commandment to honour one's parents (Exod. 20.12; Deut. 5.16) and the admonitions to children to obey parents in the New Testament household codes (Eph. 6.1–3, Col. 3.20) are addressed to minors is an adaptation to our own situation. In their original context, they were in fact addressed to adults. This means that, under Roman law, adult males could be household heads in their own right, yet owe obedience to a surviving father who legally – though usually not practically – controlled the son's property. Given much lower life expectancy than in a modern society, however, and the custom of males to marry wives as much as ten years younger than they, most adults no longer had a surviving father, though they were more likely to have a surviving mother. Wealthy Jewish, Christian and Greco-Roman widows are known to have been some of the most generous benefactors, while poor widows were some of the most vulnerable members of society. Adult children had a solemn responsibility to provide for needy widowed mothers, who otherwise had to depend on charitable aid and protection (1 Tim. 5.3–16; James 1.27).

A considerable literature on Mediterranean anthropology characterizes traditional Mediterranean cultures in terms of honour and shame as 'pivotal values'. By inference, these values are posited of their ancient counterparts as well. What this means for family life is that honour is the most precious commodity, and is always potentially under attack and must be defended. A good reputation and the respect of others – the public aspect of honour – is as important as the personal and communal integrity that inspires it. However, honour resides not principally in the individual but in the family. Males defend their own and their family's honour by their honourable behaviour with other males, their sexual prowess, *and* by protecting and controlling the women of the family, since it is the women's reputation for sexual virtue that is the most volatile element in family honour.

Women's honour in the male public world consists primarily in their reputation for respectability, and the basic component in that reputation is premarital virginity and marital exclusivity. This leads male society to view women primarily in terms of their sexual classification, and in the male perception, women's sexuality is doubly dangerous: it has the potential to seduce men but also to dishonour the family. A woman who violates the sexual code brings a shame upon her whole family that may even outlive her, and the males of her family are especially shamed because they did not prevent it. Thus the seclusion, control and subjugation of women to male authority are not only justified but internalized as proper by 'respectable' women anxious to safeguard their own honour (cf. Sir. 42.9–14; IV Macc 18.7; I Cor. 11.5–6).

In addition, the sharp distinction made between public and private life was also a gender distinction. The public world of commerce and politics belonged to men, that of the private domestic realm to women. Thus theoretically, women should be neither seen nor heard in public (I Cor. 14.34–35; I Tim. 2.11–15), while they are trusted administrators in the home (Prov. 31.10–31; notice the husband's public role in v.23). Of course, this was an upper-class ideal for those families that could afford slaves to do the outside work needed to maintain a household. Among farming peasants and urban under-classes, women had to take their place alongside men in the labour force. Yet the male orientation of the opening lines of speeches in Acts is an example of the social invisibility of women in male public rhetoric in spite of their undoubted presence in a busy market place (e.g., 3.12: *andres Israelitai*, 'male Israelites'; 2.29; 7.2, *andres adelphoi*, 'males, brothers'; 17.22, *andres Athenaioi*, 'Athenian males' – in spite of the fact that one of two named as converts as the result of the speech is a woman [v.34!]).

Only the marriages of Roman citizens came under the jurisdiction of Roman law and were recognized by it as valid marriages. Local law and custom supplied for others. Slaves were ubiquitous in Greco-Roman cities, including the households and workshops of Jews and Christians. Slave marriages existed *de facto*, but had no legal basis or protection, and partners could be separated at will by the slaves' owners. Children of these marriages could be sold at any age and thus separated from their parents. On the other hand, all evidence indicates that urban slaves had a very high expectation of gaining their freedom, usually at mid-life. But the new freedom of an adult did not transfer automatically to his or her children, who might still remain in slavery.

The lives of children in the New Testament world were precarious. Infant and childhood mortality were high, and the poor sanitation, nutrition, and health practices of the urban populace meant that many were malnourished and deprived. Methods of contraception and abortion were dangerous, arbitrary, but nonetheless practised. The most usual method of family limitation, however, was the abandonment of unwanted babies, especially daughters, who were a liability to poor families not in a position to gain in wealth and influence through their marriage. There is no way of knowing how many of these children died of exposure. But many of them were picked up by others and raised, usually as slaves. So common was this practice that there was Roman legislation about it, specifiying, for instance, that if an adult brought up in this manner could later prove free birth, he or she was to go free. Most legal systems allowed the sale of children as slaves by parents, sometimes for a limited time, sometimes indefinitely. Barbarous as it may seem, this custom often allowed those born in impoverished families to escape from starvation into an enslaved existence where at least they would survive.

The levels of access to basic education and literacy are debated by scholars, and it does seem that in many cities of the Roman period a basic literacy was fairly widespread; always, however, more so among boys than girls.[1] Primary education for those fortunate enough to have it was usually an unhappy pedagogic process in which discipline more than creative teaching was used to ensure that children learned their lessons. Paul's example of the pedagogue in Gal. 3.23–26 draws on this familiar figure in an affluent family, usually a slave, who saw to it that a boy went to school and studied his lessons.[2]

While there is no doubt that normal parents loved and were affectionate with their children, childhood was a brief period in which the children of the labouring classes and of slaves were put to work as soon as they were physically able, and the children – especially daughters – of the upper classes were married off soon after puberty in the best marriage that parents could arrange for the enhancement of family status and wealth. Jesus' pronouncement 'Unless you become like a child, you will not enter the kingdom of heaven' (Matt. 18.1–5; Mark 9.33–37; Luke 9.46–48) must have carried connotations of vulnerability and helplessness as well as innocence.

Affluent families assigned dowries to their daughters, which they brought into marriage, and at least a portion of which they expected to take back in the case of divorce. Divorce was commonly practised in both Jewish and Greco-Roman families, and divorce law, especially with regard to the consequent financial settlement, was well developed in both systems. Even when a husband administered his wife's property, he was responsible for preserving it intact, lest he had to restore it in the case of divorce. The expectation of law was that parents passed on their inheritance to their children or to members of their natal family rather than to each other, though in fact many couples deeded property to each other as well. Contrary to modern assumptions, the minor children of divorced parents were considered as belonging to their fathers, and so were much more likely to continue living with him than with their mothers. Jesus' well-documented resistance to divorce is rather surprising over against its context, either Palestinian or the later Greco-Roman environment in which these sayings were preserved (Matt. 5.31–32; 19.3–9; Mark 19.2–10; Luke 16.18; I Cor. 7.10).

Family relationships were sometimes as problematical as they are today. The figure of the father represented extraordinary legal and social power, and must have carried strong connotations of authority. Yet in real life, fathers were not necessarily the stern, distant disciplinarians that they are sometimes made out to be in stereotype.[3] The intimate yet respectful communication envisioned in the language of father and son in the Gospels, especially John, is probably a faithful reflection of the ideal father-son relationship, in which paternal authority is clearly respected, but not excessively feared. Paternal testing of sons to strengthen their character and endurance is one of the ways to understand how early Christians viewed the mystery of the suffering of God's Son (Sir. 30.1–13). Galatians 4.7 declares that all baptized believers, whether male or female, and of whatever ethnic and legal identity, are given the status of sons in the household, that is, heirs to the estate.

Fathers and daughters had a distinctly different kind of relationship. Though daughters could in certain cases inherit property apart from their dowry, they were not potential heirs of the father's status and authority in the same way that sons were. Daughters carried the potential danger of shaming the family through their misconduct or violation, and thus were a constant worry, lest they not remain virgins until marriage, lest they not please their husbands, lest a good marriage not be found for them (Sir. 42.9–14). Yet certainly a normal degree of affection existed between fathers and daughters.

The bond between mothers and sons was very close. It was by producing sons that married women gained status, and the survival and success of their sons was thus of prime importance to them. The Gospel of John's depiction of Jesus' relationship with his mother is not untypical. She remains in the background during her adult son's prominence, heard from only when necessary, yet after only a brief question at Càna, he reluctantly does what he does not want to do, because she says so (John 2.1–5). At his death, he continues to fulfil his responsibility toward his (presumably widowed) mother by providing ongoing care for her in the person of the beloved disciple (John 19.26–27).

The relationship between mothers and daughters is the least known because it is the least documented. Most literary evidence from the ancient world comes from the public world of men, and the inscriptional evidence for mothers and daughters is not abundant, either. Christian stories of exemplary women often portray them as greatly attached to their mothers, and we have no reason to conclude that normal affection was not present. In the New Testament, Salome's devotion to her mother Herodias prompted her to do without question as her mother directed her, odious as the directive must have been (Mark 6.17–29; Matt. 14.1–12), and a Gentile woman risked derision and refusal to ask Jesus for the cure of her daughter (Mark 7.24–30; Matt. 15.21–28). Yet daughters did not have the same potential for the realization of power that sons did, and, as in all patriarchal societies, daughters left their natal family to join in many senses the family of their husbands.

The relationship between mothers and their daughters-in-law, then as now, may have been one of the most difficult. Daughters were brought into their husband's house, in full view of a mother often widowed and resident, insecure about this possible shift of her son's allegiance to his wife. In view of the tight relationship between mother and son, discussed above, communications with a new wife must often have been tense. It may be significant that the three relationships to be disrupted by eschatological trials in both Micah and the Q source of the Synoptic Gospels are those between son and father, daughter and mother, and daughter-in-law and mother-in-law (Micah 7.5–6; Matt 10.34–36; Luke 12.51–53).

While the Gospel of John depicts an intimate mother-son relationship for Jesus, other Gospels give a somewhat different picture. Luke portrays Mary as a prophet who proclaims the wonderful deeds God has done through her in the conception of her son (Luke 1.46–55). Mark and Matthew present a starker scene. The first time that Jesus' relatives come seeking him, it is because he is shaming them by his conduct: 'they thought he was out of his mind' (Mark 3.21). The second time, Jesus seems to rebuff their claims by declaring all those who do God's will to be 'brother, sister, and mother' (Mark 3.31–35; Matt. 12.46–50; Luke 8.19–21). It does not seem that for Mark or Matthew, the family of Jesus, including his mother, ever become disciples. Yet what the evangelists seek to convey in this passage is that family relationship, the basis for intimacy and privileged access, in the community of Jesus no longer depends on blood or other socially established ties. Even Mary's maternity cannot be the basis of special claims on him beyond those that any disciple can make (Luke 11.27–28). The family is extended beyond conventional familial bonds, and a new basis for intimacy and mutual support is established. This new family loyalty must even take priority over traditional ones, for those who give them up will receive them a hundredfold (Matt. 19.27–29; Mark 10.28–30; Luke 18.28–30).

Beyond the setting in the life of Jesus, the Acts of the Apostles and the New Testament letters show that frequently entire families and households came together into the church, in keeping with the solidarity of families as social units and the concept of the self as part of such a unit.[4] The households of the Roman centurion Cornelius (Acts 10.44–48), the merchant Lydia (Acts 16.14–15), and an otherwise unknown Corinthian, Stephanas (I Cor. 1.16), all received baptism together. Most astounding is the story of the Philippian jail keeper who roused his family in the middle of the night to feed his distinguished visitors and accept baptism at their hands (Acts 16.32–34). In such incidents, in modern terms one wonders how much individual family members really realized what they were doing and gave consent. Yet we also know of individual converts who were not heads of households, but were received into the church on their own, especially wives of unbelieving husbands (I Cor. 7.13; I Peter 3.1), a practice that cast suspicion on Christians, Jews and other private organizations that allowed it, for it was seen to undermine the patriarchal order of the family and thus of the state.

One of the more difficult New Testament themes relating to the family concerns the so-called 'household codes', in which, principally in the Deutero-Pauline letters, the three pairs of wives-husbands, slaves-owners and children-parents are addressed in terms of mutual but unequal relationships (Eph. 5.21–6.9; Col. 3.18–4.1; partially in I Peter 2.18–3.7). The origins of this theme lie in both Jewish and Hellenistic ethics, where the well-ordered household is the microcosm of the well-ordered state. In a highly hierarchical and patriarchal culture, the fundamental equality of persons is rarely glimpsed, so it is not surprising that social order can be conceived only in terms of the leadership and control of free males over females and of elders over their children.

Beginning at least with the philosophical legacy of Plato and Aristotle, the leadership of males, as signifying rationality and intelligence, over females, as signifying sense perception and sensuality, was allegorized by male writers into the expression of the primacy of spirit over matter. Given such a paradigm, it is unthinkable that at the abstract level of ethical teaching, males and females could have been considered of equal social status (notwithstanding assertions of lack of partiality like Gal. 3.28, which in its historical context is less a declaration of social equality than a theological statement about access to salvation in Christ). Later, Christians of the fourth century onwards who glorified celibacy as the only full expression of the Christian life saw in women's celibacy their escape from the necessary link with sensuality, so that they ceased to be 'women', that is, beings whose sexuality defined them.[5]

Even if today only the vestiges of this kind of gender imaging remain, still Ephesians 5.22–33 is one of the most dangerous texts in the New Testament. Here the submission of the wife to the husband and the love of the husband for the wife are assimilated to the relationship of the church to Christ. In the ancient context of patriarchal marriage, this comparison must have been one of them most effective ways of sanctifying the marriage bond and of proposing just as challenging a role for both parties. Because of the ecclesiological comparison, however, the text has too often been seen to render normative the subordinate relationship.

There is a significant difference, however, between the New Testament household codes and most other contemporary discussion of household ordering. Whereas most ancient treatments address only the male husband-master-father and direct him how to order the family, the New Testament codes directly address all parties involved, not only the patriarchal authority, but also wives, slaves and (adult) children. This granting of personal dignity even to those who are expected to be subservient, taken together with the Christian practice of admitting wives and perhaps others to baptism outside the framework of whole household conversions, is an important hint of the direction in which Christian reflection on personhood was already leading.

No discussion of the early Christian family, however brief, can omit to stress that, in keeping with Jesus' extension of family relationship to all disciples, the early house churches saw themselves as extended families. This is clear from such evidence as the title of brothers and sisters commonly given to believers, burial in common cemeteries, and conscious modelling of community leadership on that of the household (I Tim. 3.4–5). The vision of church was that of a community that was inclusive of all, within a given culturally determined view of person in community, a view that differs considerably from ours.

The realization of the structures, ideals and flexibility of the early Christian family can lend hope to a confusing modern scene. As these structures and ideals are once more in the midst of turmoil, an awareness of the vast differences across the centuries can assure us that the present transformation is but one more step along the way, and that the family is a remarkably flexible institution that will survive and emerge, in a different shape, to be sure, but just as strong.

Notes

1. See W.V. Harris, *Ancient Literacy*, Cambridge, Massachusetts 1989.
2. The number of family images in Galatians is striking. Besides this one, the making of a will (Gal. 3.15–17); the minor status of a child (4.1–3); adoption (4.5–7); labour (4.19); and the allegory of the two wives of Abraham (4.21–31).
3. R.P. Saller, *Patriarchy, Property and Death in the Roman Family*, Cambridge Studies in Population, Economy and Society; Past Time 25, London and New York 1994.
4. B.J. Malina, '"Let Him Deny Himself" (Mark 8.34): A Social-Psychological Model of Self-Denial', *Biblical Theology Bulletin* 24, 1994, 106–19.
5. E.A. Clark, 'Ideology, History and the Construction of "Woman" in Late Ancient Christianity', *Journal of Early Christian Studies* 2, 1994, 155–84.

The History of the Family

Charles J. Reid, Jr

To understand the history of the family in Western Christendom it is necessary first to recognize that the family has changed shapes, sometimes fundamentally, over the course of two thousand years of Christian history. While the theologian may be called to articulate that which is permanent and enduring in the Christian message, it is the historian's lot to call attention to that which is time-bound and contingent. It would be overly ambitious, in the compass of this article, to try to separate the contingent from the permanent in the history of Christian marriage. Nevertheless, one can still entertain the hope that by distinguishing between the relatively permanent and the more ephemeral we might advance contemporary debate over the nature of the Christian family.

In coming to terms with the structure of Christian marriage and the family one must first understand the structure of family life found in the pagan societies that preceded it – that of the Roman Empire on the one hand, and that of the pagan 'barbarians' of Western Europe on the other.

Both the pagan Roman family and the Roman sexual ethic differed substantially from what would emerge in the fourth, fifth and sixth centuries CE as Christianity consolidated its position in the Empire. At least among the propertied elites – whose lives are better documented than their humbler contemporaries – the *familia* was the centre of domestic relations. The *familia* does not correspond to our notion of 'family'. It might best be translated as 'household', and might best be thought of as a vehicle for acquiring and conserving wealth. The *familia* comprised the wife and children of its head – the father, or *paterfamilias* – as well as slaves and other forms of property. The *paterfamilias*, however, was understood by the Roman lawyers not to be a member of the *familia*. He stood apart from it and over it. Only gradually, beginning in the third century CE, especially in the writings of such Christian authors as Tertullian, did the term *familia* come primarily to signify blood relations among its members.¹

Roman sexual ethics also differed significantly from subsequent Christian practices. Marriage was not viewed as the only legitimate outlet for sexual expression or gratification, at least where men were concerned. The sons of elites were frequently allowed and even encouraged to be sexually active during their adolescence. Prostitutes were sometimes furnished for these purposes. Young men as well often took concubines, who generally came from the lower classes of society. This practice – as St Augustine's *Confessions* attests – carried little opprobrium, at least outside Christian circles. High-born women, however, were expected to remain virgins until marriage.

Even after marriage, males were not expected to confine their sexual activity to their spouses. Recourse to prostitutes remained a socially acceptable sexual outlet, as was recourse to homosexual activity – although an elite Roman male was not expected to play the passive part in homosexual liaisons. Stoic philosophy, however, with its emphasis on impassive self-restraint, condemned the unbridled pursuit of sexual pleasure. Divorce coupled with the possibility of remarriage remained an option throughout the history of the Roman Empire. Even the Christian emperor Justinian permitted remarriage after divorce in his sixth-century reform of marriage law.²

By the end of the fifth century CE, Roman political authority in the West had largely disappeared. The primitive Germanic peoples who succeeded to Roman authority also followed a number of practices that differed substantially from Christian expectations. The records that document pagan Germanic practices – hagiography, heroic poetry, early law 'codes' – are nearly all Christian in orientation but nevertheless shed light on the pagan past. Among the Germanic tribes James Brundage identifies 'three legitimate methods of contracting marriage: by capture (*Raubehe*), by purchase (*Kaufehe*), and by mutual consent (*Friedelehe*)'.³ Concubinage was widespread and approved of, while divorce coupled with the possibility of remarriage was also allowed, especially in the first year of marriage and especially for men.

What would become the Christian approach to marriage, of course, is grounded in the first place in scriptural revelation. But the distinctive historical shape Christian marriage would take was first given decisive form in the writings of the patristic authors of the fourth and fifth centuries, especially St Jerome and St Augustine.

The patristic authors shared a background of thought and experience that had come to look with suspicion on traditional Roman sexual and marital practice and had come to exalt sexual abstinence and asceticism at the expense of active sexual expression, even within wedlock. While marriage was certainly allowed, to be perfect, it was thought, one must emulate St Antony and other such ascetics and renounce the pleasures of the flesh. Indeed, St Jerome and St Augustine both made such renunciations.

The emphasis on the superiority of the virginal, or at least the sexually continent state, over other types of life comes across especially clearly in a work like St Jerome's *Adversus Jovinianum*, which, as the title suggests, was directed against a certain Jovinian who claimed that the virginal and the married life were of equal status in God's eyes. Jerome responded with an attack which in its enthusiastic defence of the virginal state 'came close to condemning marriage'.[4]

But while marital intercourse came to be depicted as an inferior life, Catholic theologians nevertheless found it necessary to develop a theology that made room for its legitimate expression. The pre-eminent proponent of that theology would prove to be St Augustine.

Prior to his conversion to Christianity in his early thirties, St Augustine had led a life in the world as a teacher of rhetoric at Carthage, Milan and elsewhere. He took two concubines during his young adulthood and for much of this time proclaimed himself a follower of the Manichean religion, a movement which demanded that its adherents avoid procreation. This biographical detail is important where St Augustine is concerned, because much of his theology of marriage was shaped, first, by the experiences of his youth, and secondly by the polemical context of his struggle, first against Manicheism and subsequently against the confidence the Pelagian movement placed in human nature and its ability, unaided by grace, to resist the temptations of concupiscence and to achieve salvation.[5]

While St Augustine's basic attitude towards marriage, sexuality and the family can be gleaned from a number of works written over the course of forty years, his most systematic treatment is found in his treatise *De bono coniugali*, 'On the Good of Marriage'. In this work, St Augustine proposed that Christian marriage existed to serve three basic goods: procreation, fidelity and *sacramentum*, best translated as 'symbolic stability'.[6] Simultaneously, however, St Augustine proclaimed the superiority of the virginal state: ' . . . [I]t is a good to marry . . . but it is better not to marry, since it is better for human society not to have need of marriage.'[7]

The period from the sixth to the ninth century witnessed the emergence of what has been described as 'a new kind of household structure and, consequently, a new definition of the family in Western Europe'.[8] Unlike the situation that prevailed especially in pagan Rome, in which the *familia* of the elites differed considerably in structure from the unions of the humbler classes, by the time one reaches the reign of Charlemagne, '[t]he family had come to mean a co-residential, primary descent group'.[9] This was the case regardless of social class. Even so, the Christian synthesis on marriage represented by St Augustine was received only haltingly and incompletely during these centuries. Divorce and remarriage remained social realities, especially among the upper classes, as did concubinage and sexual relations outside of wedlock. Theologians and penitential writers, however, continued to keep the Augustinian vision alive, sometimes with a rigour that might have shocked even the old North African bishop.[10]

Matters changed dramatically once again beginning in the late eleventh century, with the outbreak of what has been called the 'papal revolution'.[11] The papal revolution in turn led to the growth of universities throughout Europe, a renewal of the disciplines of theology and philosophy and the birth of the new discipline of canon law. The papal revolution and its aftermath profoundly reshaped thought about sexuality and marriage. At least five aspects of the new teaching and its practical implementation require mention:

1. The virginal remained the ideal life, while married life correspondingly occupied a lesser place in the hierarchy of values. But even while canonists and theologians saw marriage as 'remedy for concupiscence', they also recognized the marital relationship as having a positive content. The canonists breathed new life into the old Roman-law expression 'marital affection', occasionally even proposing to make it into the touchstone for measuring the presence or absence of marital consent, while theologians such as Hugh of Saint Victor and Hildegard of Bingen wrote eloquently on the type of love one ought to experience within the marital relationship.

2. The Augustinian goods of marriage were defined theologically as representing basic components of the natural law and were given a prominent place in the new science of canon law. Their corollaries were also rigorously explored. Remarriage following divorce was declared impossible so long as both partners remained alive. Sexual expression was to be so conducted as not to rule out the possibility of procreation. Canonists and theologians engaged in tortured analyses of permissible and impermissible sexual postures, measured against the standard of whether procreation was possible.

3. The capacity of freely choosing one's marital partner was adopted as

normative in the first great collection of canon law, Gratian's *Decretum* (1140), and thereafter received the protection of church law. The adoption of this rule was by no means an obvious development. Neither Roman law nor Germanic law made free consent central to the formation of marriage, and Gratian himself was forced to rely on rather meagre authority to conclude in favour of freedom.[12] The new emphasis on free consent had at least two further consequences.

Canonists and theologians were forced to resolve the question whether consent or consummation made a marriage. This question was ultimately resolved in a compromise formulation of Pope Alexander III, who asserted that while consent brought a marriage into being, consummation gave it a special firmness that no earthly power could destroy.

The emphasis on consent in turn gave rise as well to the problem of clandestine marriage. Since marriage came into being when two parties exchanged present-tense consent even in the absence of witnesses, there was no completely reliable way of determining who was married. Furthermore, young people were capable of defying family wishes and marrying whom they desired, thus frustrating family plans. Court records indicate that clandestine marriage remained a pressing social problem for both of these reasons until the sixteenth century.

4. The conjugal debt came to be defined as a *right* (the *ius coniugale*) and was given the legal protection we associate with modern conceptions of rights. Even though the mediaeval family was in many respects a hierarchical and 'patriarchal' structure, the conjugal debt served as a means of equalizing the relationship. It was a claim-right either party could assert, and the other party was not free to deny. The canonists attempted to defend this right against third-party interference (feudal lords, for example, were called upon to respect the conjugal rights of their serfs), and popes proclaimed their powerlessness to abrogate the rights of parties to a consummated, Christian marriage.[13]

5. Finally, the canonists constructed a judicial system to oversee and regulate the marital conduct of the Christians of Western Europe. Although Jewish law had long claimed jurisdiction over the marriages of people of the Hebraic faith, the church was able to put the full weight of public authority behind its claims. This was a novel accomplishment. As Richard Helmholz has observed: 'The problem was to ensure that ordinary marriage disputes went to any court at all. The real hurdle was the persistent idea that people could regulate marriages for themselves. The disappearance of this idea occurred gradually, over a very long period of time.'[14]

Much of the scholastic-canonistic synthesis which these five points represent was challenged frontally by the Protestant reformers. Martin Luther rejected the exalted status given the virginal state. In Lutheran theology, 'holy matrimony' was to be exalted, and the celibate state rejected as scripturally unjustified and humanly unsustainable. Luther and the Reformers also rejected the primacy the canonists placed on consent in marital formation, and attacked clandestine marriage as the sin of disobedience to one's parents. Luther, followed by the other Reformers, also recognized remarriage after divorce as permissible in at least some circumstances.[15]

Western Catholicism responded to the Reformers' attack at the Council of Trent, which accepted a portion of the Reformers' agenda, but also rejected a part of it. Trent rejected efforts to declare the virginal and married states equal (a position finally adopted by the Second Vatican Council), and restated the traditional Catholic position against remarriage following divorce. The Council did, however, take to heart Luther's attack on clandestine marriage, effectively outlawing the practice in the decree *Tametsi*, which declared invalid marriages not performed before a priest and two witnesses.

The modern world of the late twentieth century now poses a whole series of challenges to both Roman Catholic and Protestant syntheses. Some writers even speak of our living in a 'post-marriage' society. The legal systems of most Western countries that once assisted in the enforcement of the traditional ideal no longer provide positive support for marriage understood in conformity with the Augustinian goods of marriage. Symbolic stability goes unmentioned in modern legal analysis, divorce is widely available and procreation receives only halting public recognition as a purpose to marriage. It is socially acceptable to engage in sexual intercourse outside wedlock, while new technologies facilitate contraception and abortion.

At the same time, however, new insights – such as psychological studies on the nature of human affection – have helped us achieve a deeper awareness of some aspects of the matrimonial relationship. Along these lines, one of the more remarkable developments in contemporary canon law has been the adoption by the Roman Rota beginning in the 1950s and 1960s of psychological standards for measuring the validity of marital consent. In the decades ahead, we will no doubt witness many more such creative responses to contemporary challenges.

The history that has been sketched above may, it is hoped, serve as a sort of touchstone for future reflection on the direction of Christian marriage and the family. At least four concluding observations are in order:

1. Christian conceptions of marriage and the family took root in societies that accepted as normative family relationships very different from what we take as appropriate. In the process of taking root and flourishing, the Christian vision entirely supplanted these older conceptions.

2. The Christian vision of marriage and the family has not been a static one. Certain features once assumed to be permanent – such as the hierarchical superiority of the virginal over the married state – have now been discarded. Other features – such as the requirement to marry before a priest and two witnesses – have been added.

3. The traditional Christian vision of marriage is not necessarily hostile to modern trends. Indeed, the synthesis that took shape in the eleventh, twelfth and thirteenth centuries provides important intellectual roots to such seemingly modern developments as the necessity that parties consent freely to marriage, the belief that marriage should be a relationship of equality between the parties (found originally in canonistic speculation on the *ius coniugale*), and the desire to see marriage as a means by which the parties to it might achieve mutual fulfilment (traceable to theorizing on the content of 'marital affection').

4. Nevertheless, since the fifth century, the Augustinian goods of marriage have provided at least the Roman Catholic Church with a basic organizational framework for structuring analyses of marriage. The Augustinian goods also remain the foundation of the canon law of marriage. How this framework is used and adapted to respond to contemporary and future developments may be one of the most important issues facing us today.

Notes

1. Even so, David Herlihy, *Medieval Households*, Cambridge, MA 1985, 3, notes that '[t]here is no implication in either the Christian or the pagan writing that this *familia* represented a coresidential unit, with its own moral identity'.

2. On Roman social ethics see James A. Brundage, *Law, Sex, and Christian Society in Medieval Europe*, Chicago 1987, 22–49; on Roman divorce see John T. Noonan Jr, 'Novel 22,' in *The Bond of Marriage*, ed. William W. Bassett, Notre Dame, Ind. 1968, 41–96.

3. See Brundage, *Law, Sex, and Christian Society in Medieval Europe*, (n.2), 128. Marriage by consent, Brundage suggests, was the least favoured of the three possibilities: 'A man who did *not* wish to risk the legal and physical hazards of abduction and who was either too poor, too powerless, or too mean to purchase a bride had the alternative of marrying by consent' (129).

4. Ibid., 85. See also Dyan Elliott, *Spiritual Marriage: Sexual Abstinence in Medieval Wedlock*, Princeton 1993, 43–4.

5. For the relationship of St Augustine's life to his theology see especially John T. Noonan Jr, *Contraception: A History of Its Treatment by the Catholic Theologians and Canonicists*, Cambridge, MA 1966, 119–26. On Augustine and the Pelagians see ibid., 131–5.

6. Ibid., 127–8.

7. See St Augustine, *The Good of Marriage (De bono coniugale)*, Vol. 15, The Fathers of the Church, Washington DC, 1955, 22.

8. See Brundage, *Law, Sex, and Christian Society in Medieval Europe* (n.2), 134.

9. Ibid.

10. See Brundage's discussion of the penitential literature, ibid., 152–69.

11. This was the contest between Gregory VII and Henry IV. See generally Harold J. Berman, *Law and Revolution: The Formation of the Western Legal Tradition*, Cambridge, MA 1983.

12. See John T. Noonan Jr, 'Power to Choose', *Viator* 4, 1973, 419–34.

13. See Charles J. Reid Jr, 'The Canonistic Contribution to the Western Rights Tradition: An Historical Inquiry', *Boston College Law Review* 33, 1991, 80–91.

14. See Richard H. Helmholz, *Marriage Litigation in Medieval England*, Cambridge 1974, 5.

15. On the Reformation approach to marriage and sexuality, see Brundage, *Law, Sex, and Christian Society in Medieval Europe* (n.2); see also John Witte Jr, 'The Reform of Marriage Law in Martin Luther's Germany: Its Significance Then and Now', *The Journal of Law and Religion* 4, 1986, 1–59.

Forms of Cohabitation and Procreation Outside Marriage

Rinus Houdijk

Technological developments intervene deeply in our human life and society, as can be clearly seen, for example, from the ever-new medical and technical possibilities in health care. New knowledge is constantly being acquired, and at the same time new forms of treatment are appearing: the one leads to the other. There is, however, a fundamental ambiguity about such technological developments. This becomes evident from the effects that they have: on the one hand there is a positive, healthy aspect, as with the prolongation of life; and on the other there is a negative, unhealthy aspect, for example the postponement of someone's 'natural' death. But the ambiguity goes deeper than the level of effects: at the present stage of developments, it also relates to the very foundations of technology. May some technological possibilities really be explored any further, for example genetic manipulation in human beings? From the perspective of justice mustn't the means available be devoted at an earlier stage and to a greater degree to general health care rather than to a highly specialized and élitist form of medical techniques?

In the sphere of sexuality and procreation, the technical means of contraception, of which the condom and 'the pill' are the best known and most easily available, have come to be almost taken for granted in the Western world, although they are really quite recent. The very fact that procreation has been structurally detached from the act of love between man and woman is of historic importance for the forms of cohabitation of men and women. In marriage, and outside it, the sexual union of man and woman is now primarily judged by its personal and erotic significance, and procreation now has 'only' the status of added value, when this is expressly desired. Moreover, the sexual union of man and woman no longer calls for the institution of marriage as a matter of course: where there is no longer necessarily the prospect of children, the evident a priori need for the social institution of marriage no longer exists. Furthermore, the priority of the personal and erotic element in the experience of sexuality has contributed to the recognition of forms of cohabitation outside marriage, up to and including homosexual relationships. Both these forms of cohabitation and traditional marriage now face the task of giving a humane form to the 'new' sexual relationships.

Where sexuality has been technically detached from procreation, the opposite also happens: procreation is technically detached from sexuality. This, too, is a historic event, which fundamentally changes human life and human society. The fact that sperm and ovum can be brought together outside an act of love between a man and a woman raises the question of the link between procreation and sexual intercourse between a man and a woman. It also raises the question of the link between procreation and identity. Does someone who comes into the world have to have his or her own biologically identifiable father and mother? This similarly raises the question of the milieu in which the child lives: does a child need to grow up in a 'family' in which parents (possibly only for social reasons) consist of a father and a mother, or can a form of cohabitation be sufficient in which there is only one parent (a man or woman), or the parents are two men or two women? Finally, it poses a question to society as a whole: will society maintain that procreation remains a matter for individuals, or will it increasingly hand procreation over to technological institutes and scientific experts which want to work only with the 'procreative material' that they take from selected men and women?

1. Procreative technology and forms of society

Donum vitae: *yes, provided that, and no, unless*

When the Instruction of the Congregation for the Doctrine of Faith, *Donum vitae*, on respect for the beginning of human life and the dignity of procreation, appeared in 1987, it did not receive a particularly warm welcome in my country, the Netherlands, even from many loyal Catholics who felt ties to the church. One reason for this, of course, was a general reason which applies to almost all recent official Vatican documents, namely that they present themselves so apodictically as the last word which is not open to further discussion. But it was not warmly received in particular because of the specific fact that the instruction described even *in vitro* fertilization of the gametes of partners who are joined together in marriage as morally reprehensible. A woman who is still young, who had a good Catholic upbringing and is still a regular churchgoer, living a monogamous life in a wedding solemnized in church and who so far has been unable to have a child told me of her indignation at the fact that the attempts by her and her husband to have children through *in vitro* fertilization were being condemned by the (official) church. They felt deeply hurt by this both as human beings and as Catholic Christians, coming as it did on top of their having to submit to the technical medical procedures required, which they had experienced as no less than a way of suffering. Here, it might be remarked in passing, one comes up against the appalling alienation which the present-day rigoristic morality of the official church results in among many of its faithful believers. How are we to understand the argument of *Donum vitae* on the position mentioned?

The argument is that homologous artificial fertilization objectively brings about a division between the two significant features of the 'act of marriage', namely marital union and an orientation on procreation. It is argued that artificial fertilization aims at procreation which is not the fruit of the specific act of marital union. Looked at more closely, the Instruction argues that the two significant features mentioned must be present *in the act*, that the *full* significances must be realized separately in any 'marital act', and that a child which is born has to be conceived in a biologically natural sexual act of the married couple. Here, of course, we see the whole problem arising which is posed by the act-morality of the moral doctrine of the official Catholic Church generally: despite its emphatic talk about the human person, the end-result of such morality seems to be not personalistic but naturalistic (F. Böckle). My own view is that on the question of homologous artificial fertilization the starting point must not be the abstract demands of a particular doctrine; I fear that the underlying concern of the institution is not to endanger the validity of church teaching about abortion and *Humanae Vitae*, and that makes it blind to reality. In my view, the ethical assessment must begin with the position (not the interests) of the possible future child. In that case it seems that according to *personal* criteria this child is born of the marital love of its parents, which is also attested physically; that according to *social* criteria the child comes into the world in a stable community of husband and wife, with family, friends and acquaintances; and that there is a more than usual certainty according to criteria of *biological identity*. In this case it is merely a 'defect of nature' (infertility) that is being corrected by human intervention, of the kind that we treat so much and, rightly, so in accordance with the creaturely task which has been given to human beings.

Technology and nature

However, it should be noted that here in my criticism of the Instruction on the specific point of homologous artificial fertilization I am utilizing some basic principles of church teaching itself, which I am adopting. What principles are these? If we leave aside the dominant ideological interest (establishing its own truth and the claims to power bound up with it), then we can recognize in the Instruction a Leitmotif to which I myself would want sincerely to subscribe (in what follows I am not giving a summary account, but my own reconstruction of the text).

The most important basic principle for today's technological world is that human procreation is a matter for human beings themselves (physically), and may not be taken over by technology and technological institutions. The statement of this principle is not addressed primarily to individual men and women in their individual situations but primarily envisages society as a whole. Moreover, this statement is not made from a biologistic perspective (as seems to be the case in the Instruction), but relates to society and institutional structure. Just as human procreation is not a matter for the state (although here the state has a particular responsibility), so too it may not become a matter for anonymous scientific institutes and technological laboratories. Human procreation must remain a matter for human beings themselves, with their own physical and psychological conditions and their own cultural differences, so that the 'natural history' of the succession of the generations is continued. Technological intervention into human procreation may make whole and support, but it can never replace human beings themselves. This starting point also implies that limits must be set to the 'utopia' which is inherent in technology and which is itself unbounded.

In the meantime, the 'technicalization' of contraception and procreation is the basis of the possibility of all kinds of new forms of activities in connection with sexuality and procreation. Thus with the availability of technical means of contraception, within traditional marriage, too, the sexual intercourse of the couple is in principle no longer burdened by the fate of possible pregnancy, and there, too, in principle a guaranteed planning of births has been made possible. Moreover, even the 'natural' methods of birth control allowed by the church's magisterium presuppose the moral legitimacy of birth control ('responsible parenthood'): in the political debate over population growth this fact seems to be being buried. However, the use of technical means in connection with human procreation is far more problematical. Artificial insemination in its different forms, *in vitro* fertilization and embryo transfer, and all such technical possibilities, put us in the position on the one hand of treating sperm and ovum as 'biological material' on which technical operations can be performed and into which experimental scientific investigation can be carried out (that falls outside the scope of this article), and on the other of achieving pregnancy outside the familiar framework of the traditional marriage. Thus it is possible to become pregnant by artificial insemination by donor; sperm and ovum can be brought together *in vitro* and subsequently implanted in a woman volunteer so that a child is born through a surrogate mother. Such technical possibilities are not available neutrally, in a purely instrumental capacity, but are embedded in a social and cultural field of force in which the utopian delusion of technology already mentioned has a reciprocal effect on the day-dreams of the 'myth of self-fulfilment' and vice versa.

A distinction needs to be made. If 'self-fulfilment' stands for the integral development of the person, for cultural and social emancipation, and for self-control in the sphere of morality on the basis of a trained conscience, then the criterion of self-fulfilment is an ethically legitimate one. But if what we have is the 'myth' of self-fulfilment, then we have boundless desires and delusions in which everything quite indiscriminately is made to depend on the satisfaction of personal needs. The need itself then becomes a defining criterion for moral choice. And that is also the suggestion which is constantly made through advertising and the media in Western consumer society: follow your needs, otherwise you won't be happy. Sometimes the mere reference to an existing need (for example, the existence of the desire for a child) is thought sufficient in itself to legitimate a particular action. But moral judgment must not be put under the yoke of the economic criterion of need; it must submit to the test of justice and what is truly good.

The domination of economic thinking in moral questions within the context of our present-day Western society is given fundamental expression once again in what one can call an economic approach to the question of having children (both within 'traditional' marriage and outside it). Whether or not to have a child is made to depend very much on an economic calculation. First, does having a child fit in with the personal well-being and personal aspirations of the potential parent(s)? And secondly, will the future child be of such a 'quality' as to correspond sufficiently to the wishes of its parent(s) – and, implicitly, also to the wishes of society as a whole? The more account is taken of this 'requirement of quality', the more the hold of society and the technological institutes over procreation will increase. In my view, this social fact needs to be the main topic of present-day ethical reflection on procreation and forms of society, rather than individualized problems of infertility or parenthood. Even then, it is probably inevitable that theology will try, without excluding any therapeutic intervention (not eugenics) which may possibly be necessary, to keep alive the notion that a child is a gift that must be expected for its own sake. But that is not enough. Public discussion needs to be encouraged on the question of the right relationship between technology and human nature.

Classical ethics once made a distinction between technique (*techne*) as the action of human beings themselves, and nature (*physis*), that which has an intrinsic motive principle. *Physis* remains outside the grasp of human beings. In the framework of present-day technological society, how to use this distinction is a question of the first order, not least in the case of human procreation. The question need not be answered in an absolute sense and for all times, but it must be discussed constantly in society and the church. It must constantly be raised afresh, and answered, though the answers given will be provisional ones. Perhaps at this stage we cannot do much more than raise questions and indicate topics for discussion. That is what I shall do here, following the line of some basic principles of *Donum vitae*.

A human child may never be the product of a technological institute, but must come from living human beings who are concerned for it. A human child is born, not produced; and it comes into the world in a social sphere of love and care.

Children need to be born into a situation in which they stand in an identifiable succession of generations. In passing, it should be noted that it must be possible to demonstrate biological fatherhood as such precisely after the event. Individuals must know their origin, by convention, for the social reason mentioned above of having a recognizable name and descent. Social identity has priority over (presumed) biological identity. And, also in passing, this topic is not a question of condemning individual instances of e.g. artifical insemination by donor; it is a question of safeguarding the social institution of human procreation.

A human child has the right to a father and a mother, from whose love it is born. Here, too, the aim is not to condemn individual instances of one-parent families or to suggest that children with one known parent will *per se* be unhappy (which is not the case). The issue is one of the *social importance* of children as a rule being entrusted to a (stable) parental couple, and the anthropological importance of a human child being born from the love of two people which is also attested physically. In passing: *Donum vitae* thinks that a child must also *per se* come from a *de facto* 'natural' sexual act (that is the basis of its rejection of homologous *in vitro* fertilization). However, in my view, this is naturalism. The issue is the love between two people who together want a child, a love which is also attested physically.

A human child must by preference be born in a stable relationship between two people who love one another. This stability has the advantage of providing the social benefit of a stable environment in which the child can be brought up.

II. Normativity and physical nature

Veritatis splendor: *nuancing a theme*

In the encyclical *Veritatis splendor* (nos. 48–50), one can read passages which put a strong emphasis on the fact that human beings are persons and as such form an inner unity of spirit and body (*anima et corpore unus*). This fact, which is indeed so central to the Catholic tradition and characteristic of it, leads the encyclical to state that even the bodily nature of human beings is also morally relevant. In concrete terms, the encyclical seeks to show that 'natural tendencies' (*inclinationes naturales*) also have an ethical relevance, because and in so far as they relate to the human person.

It seems to me that theology has to subscribe to these basic affirmations. The problem is that in *Veritatis splendor* they appear in a context in which the accusation of a biologistic and naturalistic argument is rejected, but in which such an argument is used in the rejection of '(artificial) contraception, direct sterilization, masturbation, sexual relations before marriage, homosexual relations and artificial fertilization' (no.47).

The ethical relevance of corporeality

Human beings are also *physis*, natural beings made up of body and soul. In this sense there can be no ethical reflection on human beings without 'natural morality' of humanity. I have already made a distinction between a morality of the 'first' nature and a morality of the 'second' nature. The morality of the first nature defines human beings either as natural beings characterized by anthropological constants or by scientifically established determinations (modern anthropological moral systems of all kinds), or as natural beings with a metaphysical structure (like Neo-Scholastic Catholic moral theology). However, the morality of the 'second nature' recognizes the modern understanding of human beings as subjectivity and personality, within which in a specifically human way individuality, sociality and the nature of being human are combined with a recognition of the technological and emancipatory dimensions of modern rationality. But at the same time it recognizes the natural conditions (not determinations) of human life, without which human life ceases to be human. So we already saw that human procreation may not be expropriated by technological apparatuses in the bodies of loving people. Consequently a morality of the 'second nature' means that in everything related to our body (procreation, sexuality, eating and drinking, hygiene, sport and body culture) there must be a quest for ways of removing the body from the compulsive image-making of postmodern society, an image-making which alienates us from our own bodies by manipulation. A morality of the 'second nature' refuses above all to see the human body and human life generally as a value, just as 'goods' on the market represent an economic exchange value. The human body and human life have an intrinsic significance, may be there for their own sake, and therefore need to be respected and cherished 'for nothing'.

Translated by John Bowden

The Psychology of Family Relationships

Sidney Callahan

Psychology and moral theology

Psychology is such a huge and splintered field that it can barely be considered a single discipline. At this point different research psychologists are studying a range of topics using different theoretical models, different research methods and focussing on different levels of analysis. Today psychologists study brain mechanisms, inherited temperament, personality structures, learning, cognition, emotion, sexuality, language development, the life cycle, therapeutic clinical change, moral development and other factors in social, group and cross-cultural interactions. At the same time huge numbers of applied psychologists devote their efforts to therapeutic clinical practice or evaluative consultations with institutions and industrial organizations.

Psychology as a sprawling secular discipline stands at one end of the spectrum of inquiry near biology, medicine and neuroscience and at the other pole shares interests with sociology, anthropology and philosophy. Hundreds of different psychological organizations and professional journals go their separate ways with few attempts at integration. Yet it is also safe to say that despite the diversity of approaches in psychology, most psychologists would consider the institution of the family to be the dominant influence in forming the individual and affecting the larger society.

In its affirmation of the family as centrally important, psychology converges with Christian theological teaching which also insists that the family is vital for religious formation, religious practice and the general well-being of society. A good working definition of the family can be found in a statement of the US bishops, who describe the family as 'an intimate community of persons bound together by blood, marriage or adoption for the whole of life'. This core definition is a prototype of what constitutes a family, although other kinds of families may exist.

Psychological insights into family relationships and theological reflection on the family can be mutually illuminating. Moral theologians can learn about families from psychological findings, and many psychologists may find in theology a normative framework and committed moral values which a secular discipline of psychology cannot provide.

Psychology, whether it is considered to be a hard science, a social science or an interpretative human science, remains a descriptive inquiry rather than a morally prescriptive project. Even clinical applications of psychology should properly remain remedial, rather than claiming a moral mandate of quasi-spiritual authority. Most mainstream psychologists deplore the fact that popular psychologists and new-age enthusiasts overstep the limits of the discipline. Although certain basic values always inform any scientific or therapeutic human endeavour, secular psychology by itself cannot provide the moral foundation for family life or be the source of theological guidance.

No amount of data on how individuals or families function or define themselves can generate definitive moral conclusions about how families *ought* to function. To be morally prescriptive you must go beyond empirical findings and clinical practice and make moral arguments using moral reasoning grounded on moral or theological foundations. Yet psychological findings and theories can offer moral theology vital experiential bases for reflection, as well as providing negative examples from clearly evident dysfunctions and breakdowns.

But such a psychological task is difficult because no psychological theory or basic paradigm has as yet been adopted by everyone working in the field. Psychologists regularly ask whether this is because psychology is such a young science in a pre-paradigmatic stage of development or, as seems more likely, because of the inherent complexity of the subject matter. After all, psychology, unlike chemistry or biology, attempts to study a rational 'self-interpreting animal' who can consciously initiate actions affecting self, others and the environment, while being in turn continually affected by an ever-changing environment.

In such an open recursive system of interpretations and reflexive interacting influence there is room for Catholic moral theologians to engage in faith-based interpretations of the family grounded in reason informed by faith. Morally helpful reflection on the family can best be created by combining psychological findings, theological insights and moral reasoning. Psychology for its part offers an overwhelming array of material.

Psychologies of family relationships

If psychology has a unique approach to the family, it lies in its emphasis upon the inner life and inter-personal functionings of the family over time. Psychology explores why and how persons process information, how they appropriate beliefs, how they come to feel certain emotions and moral obligations that lead to familial behaviour. Processes of direct socialization and overt communication in a family go on constantly, but for psychologists other factors are also at work that do not always include awareness. Every psychological model posits some form of implicit, covert, pre-conscious processes that shape individuals and families.

Of course external forces within a society will also play a large and determining part in any specific family's life. Shared cultural beliefs and accepted norms about who counts as a family and how family life should be conducted will exert normative pressures on behaviour. Economics, politics and natural forces will also determine a particular family's functioning. Wars, depressions, droughts, famines, diseases and natural disasters shape a family's historical environment as surely as the kind of medical technologies and working conditions available to the family. But all of the larger forces operating in a particular era or locale will still be filtered, interpreted, mediated and acted upon through the active psychological processes of interacting individual family members.

What are some of these processes? Psychologists studying the family can focus on different levels of human functions and take different time-frames for the units of analysis. Evolutionary psychologists take the long-term view and are interested in how the human family developed within the genetic evolution of the human species. In the process they study the psychic unity of humankind developing as one species over time. What psychological capacities are necessary for kinship bonds, extended nurturing, symbolic language use and group socialization, and what familial traits and characteristics will affect genetic success and selection? Such psychological inquiry is influenced by socio-biologists who see genetic influence as pre-consciously determining the basic nature of the family. A genetic drive is postulated which impels organisms to reproduce and get their genes into the next generation.

In this perspective inherent genetic programmes produce a primary biological drive toward mating, gender differentiation, reproductive strategies, parental caretaking, infant attachment, altruism, playfulness, dominance hierarchies, competition, aggression and self-deception within the social group. In other words, to understand the inner life of any family you must understand evolutionary genetics and the unconsciously active pressures of selection.

Theories of evolutionary psychology can be seen as helpful in understanding the sexual and reproductive basis of families, but they tend to pay less attention to the many other universal psychological programmes that shape human beings. Today some of the most exciting research findings emphasize the influence of mind and consciousness in shaping bodily organic functioning and health. Certainly, from infancy on the brain's neuronal development, structure and biochemistry is influenced by the amount and kinds of cognitive stimulation and affective social experiences encountered. The complexity of the mutual interactions (bottom-up and top-down) in the mind/brain/body unit has yet to be fathomed or fully understood – but it is recognized as the newest frontier of psychology and medicine.

Psychoanalytic psychologies also have recognized the complexity of the human organism and emphasized the ways that unconscious biological and instinctual forces interact with early family experiences. Today, much of orthodox Freudian theory has been reinterpreted or displaced, but there remain many different schools of thought identifying themselves with the psychoanalytic tradition – such as that of object relations, ego psychology or self psychology. Jungian and transpersonal depth psychologies have moved such a distance from the original psychoanalytic model that they have become more aligned with religious inquiry than with mainstream academic psychology.

Within the remaining psychoanalytic traditions there exist many conflicting claims, but some highly probable conclusions may be drawn from this huge body of work. While the orthodox Freudian Oedipal story of sex, aggression and death instincts may no longer be accepted as gospel truth, there does seem to be converging evidence that the earliest experiences between babies and caretakers within the family configuration influence a person's later inter-personal relationships. And of course conflict, frustration, aggression, competition, dangerous desires, illusions, ambivalence, loss and mourning are part of every human story and family narrative.

It makes sense to accept the fact that a great deal of pre-verbal learning takes place before a child can talk. Those who try to remember their childhood realize that individuals have experiences which cannot be consciously recalled in adulthood. These early family interactions appear to produce internalized patterns of critical core interpersonal relationships in memory which without awareness shape later expectations and social interactions. For instance, it is important for a child to internalize an implicit basic trust in the reliability of people and the goodness of the world. Some theorists would even say that an individual's implicit unconscious images of God have been created by early childhood experience of one's mother or father.

At any rate, most psychologists would agree that one can possess implicit assumptions about relationships with other persons that remain operative outside of full self-awareness. Today psychologists are still interested in the unconscious, but the greatest interest is on the cognitive unconscious, or the complex processes of selective attention, memory storage and retrieval of information.

Unfortunately some early internalized family experiences and expectations stored in memory may be maladaptive for coping with later encounters. The psychoanalytic claim, taken up by many subsequent psychotherapies, has been that when unnoticed, unaware, preconscious or unconscious maladapted personal patterns of functioning are attended to and emerge into conscious awareness there is an opportunity for an individual, or a family, to change. New insights into the self's habitual self-self or self-other relationships can be gained through corrective emotional experiences in a new relationship – often found in psychotherapy. New ways of thinking and new ways of feeling can be internalized in an intimate trusting relationship that directs attention to problematical interactions. In a sense psychotherapy provides a positive correction or supplement for an individual's original family formation.

Many new forms of psychotherapy have developed within clinical psychology, and much evidence exists to show that many different types of therapy can work in improving individual and family functioning. Therapies have many characteristics in common that produce re-education and positive changes in thoughts, feelings and behaviour. Fortunately, families that have provided what has been called an 'average expectable environment' of enough nurture and structural support will have ensured that their children can cope with stress. If family strengths and good family communication exists in a favourble environment, family members develop their own built-in self-corrective therapeutic processes.

But the psychosocial factors in a family are not the whole picture. There is a new realization in psychology that innate genetic factors, along with prenatal conditions, can affect a child in ways that parents cannot control. An earlier era saw the infant as a *tabula rasa*, but no longer. Today, it is recognized that a child inherits a particular temperament and specific potentialities for different kinds of intelligences, along with his or her physiological characteristics. Unfortunately, children also can have a predisposition for certain mental disorders. In an earlier day families were often falsely blamed for causing their children's mental illnesses through bad parenting (usually bad mothering) within pathologically skewed families. Today many of the same dysfunctions, such as autism, would be attributed to innate biochemical or brain dysfunctions.

It has also become clear that parents do not control the innate programmes of cognitive, linguistic and emotional development that naturally flower in average or good enough families. Children learn to speak, think, play and reason in incredible manifestations of rule-governed intelligence. Innately programmed emotional developments produce a child ready to feel and express positive and negative emotions in the course of family experience. Love, joy, interest, shame, guilt, sadness, anger, contempt and disgust appear, along with other more subtle emotional combinations.

Interactive processes of thinking and feeling make it possible, even easy, for children to be socialized into the family culture. Moral development, aesthetic development, religious development, logical development – all appear to be universal pan-species characteristics that individuals develop within the matrix of family living. The bonds of affection and the processes of identification with trustworthy adults are particularly important for cognitive-affective moral development in which one not only learns moral standards of worth but cares enough for people to want to be good.

Developmental psychologists try to understand how all the different potentialities of human beings emerge and change. There is an attempt to integrate biological development, cognitive-emotional development, sexual and social roles along with religious and moral development. Of course, in the process behavioural learning and environmental contingencies play a large part in each individual's developmental story.

While reductionist and radical behaviourist theories have lost credibility in a psychology transformed by computers, informational sciences and a general 'cognitive revolution', behaviourist learning principles are accorded respect. They have been incorporated into behaviour therapies and into other biological, cognitive and developmental approaches. In fact a new cognitive-behavioural approach to therapy pays attention to the conditioning of reward and punishment as well as to the effects of thinking or habitual self-talk.

In the narrative of every life there is an interplay of contingent conditioning along with individual self-determination. Happily, existential psychologists influenced by philosophy never accepted either behaviourist or psychoanalytical determinism and kept their focus on the conscious self's freedom of choice and search for meaning. Self-consciousness and self-control can affect innate biological and cognitive programmes as well as shape the individual's unique environment. Human beings are always simultaneously acting and being acted upon from infancy to old age.

At first developmental psychology focussed upon infants, children and adolescents. Interest then extended to the psychology of adulthood, its passages and transitions. With an ever-increasing population of old persons, the psychology of old age and dying has become a psychological and psychiatric specialty. Certain developmental patterns appear to be pan-specific, but of course different cultures also affect the way individuals progress through the life-cycle. Indeed, cross-cultural psychology or ethnopsychology focuses its inquiries into the psychological effects on individuals and families of variations in culture.

Many developmental psychologists taking inspiration from both sociology and anthropology began to study the developmental life-cycle of the family. Every new family must be founded, go through different stages of expansion and then cope with the death of its members and the rise of a new generation. Yet the formation of the individual and the family is always intimately affected by relationships to outsiders, such as peer groups, colleagues, neighbours and other institutional authorities. Ecological environmental psychological models of development have been formulated to try to analyse the interacting influence of individuals, family members, peers, other social groupings and even the physical environment.

One of the newest psychological approaches to the family is an ecological systems approach. The family is seen as a system, a whole configuration which is more than the sum of its members. The family system is engaged in maintaining itself in an operating equilibrium. As in a hanging mobile, when one element in the system changes the rest of the system must automatically realign itself. But change is often resisted since the family system has emerged in the first place to maintain order and predictability.

The family systems approach has engendered many new approaches to psychological interactions in the family. Some theories focus on communication within the family system, or on the amount of openness or rigidity of boundaries in the various family sub-systems, such as the parents or the siblings. Will the family system be both flexible and stable enough to meet the inevitable challenges that will arise?

The present operating system of a family is always seen to be influenced by patterns passed on from earlier generations. Inter-generational patterns repeat themselves and can be either adaptive or maladaptive; they can also be reproduced in a family system without explicit awareness. Once again the factors that shape the inside story of the family can be outside explicit consciousness. Therapeutic interventions in family therapy are aimed at changing the family system so that dysfunctional patterns can be interrupted and existing family strengths activated. Conscious awareness may or may not be necessary for change in a family system.

In sum, no matter what the level of psychological analysis, psychological approaches emphasize the importance of family processes. The species-specific human genetic heritage comes into play through sexual reproduction. But innate human developmental programmes cannot fulfil their potential except through family nurture and emotionally invested caretaking. Every touch, every emotional attunement or misattunement, every conversation, every exercise of power or discipline, every direct and indirect communication within the family builds up a unique personality in a unique family. How does the family celebrate, worship, play, laugh, fight or mourn together? What ritual norms of etiquette are demanded? The patterning of micro-events creates larger narratives. Individual character and family histories are enacted moment by moment in a multitude of choices and responses.

The way communication, power, authority, conflict, gender, roles and decision-making are handled in the family of origin have ramifications for all later social groups that a person enters. A template for group or social interaction is acquired. One's attitude towards civic and religious authorities is partially shaped by the original pattern of family governance. Those worried about totalitarian tendencies or intolerance in a culture have seen a correlation between democratic families and democratic societies.

The study of history and a perusal of today's news reveal the sad truth that families often fail to fulfil a nurturing or supportive role. Today we see problems of neglect, immaturity and inadequacy, as well as despicable abuses of power such as incest, violent battering and mental cruelty. Since the emotional stakes are so high, family members can be exceedingly destructive to one another. When families operate within relative privacy and isolation, and with little community support, oportunities for unchecked aggression increase. Too often one member, usually male, perhaps under the influence of drugs or alcohol, will abuse the more vulnerable and dependent family members. The power of the family to further human flourishing and happiness guarantees that it can also become a kind of hell on earth.

By contrast, when the family fulfils its potential for mutual love and support, its members can have a sense of meaning and ascribed status that need not be earned. Irreversible biological kinship ties connect families through time and space. In having parents and grandparents, as well as collateral kin, each child can discern the existence of a transcendent community existing beyond the individual subject. The family potently imparts implicit and explicit lessons of cultural, moral and religious norms; these norms are socially validated as real and obligatory. The flourishing of families is crucial for the continuation of civilization and religious belief.

Moral and theological reflection on the psychology of family relationships

Understanding the powerful formative influence of the family's psychological relationships induces moral theologians to urge support for families by both church and state. All of the positive innate psychological predispositions of family interactions, such as love, kinship bonding, altruism, co-operation and mutual support and comfort should be encouraged and affirmed as morally worthy.

At the same time the inevitability of sin must be recognized. Moral warnings and admonitions should be issued against harmful family tendencies such as aggressive abuse of power, selfish exploitation, competitiveness, careless neglect, regression and selfish inertia. The moral and theological message of the gospel teachings must be clearly applied to the family. A good family practises love, justice and equality among its members and towards its neighbours. Psychologically, moral freedom and moral responsibility are affirmed as the bases for making permanent promises and responsible reproductive decisions. Loving families through mutual correction and aspiration to greater love can become effective schools of virtue; they advance social well-being through the practice of hospitality and service to the world.

A family as the church in the home can be the world turned inside out; in Christian community those with authority and power serve others, and all work together for the common good. In a good family the strong take care of the vulnerable and dependent members, be they unborn, young, old, ill, handicapped or dying. Mutual love and just care can overcome sinful practices of abuse, exploitation, selfishness or gender discrimination in the family.

The family as the domestic church creates, sustains and passes on the faith to its members. Through implicit and explicit communication, by example and by ritual, new members are inducted into a form of life. As a mediating institution the family, like the church, must build up its own inner community and turn outward to transform the world. Love is the goal of the family mission and love is the way.

Bibliographical References

Articles

John F. Kihlstrom, 'The Cognitive Unconscious', *Science*, 18 September 1987, 1445–52

Elizabeth F. Loftus and Mark R. Klinger, 'Is the Unconscious Smart or Dumb?', *American Psychologist*, June 1992, Vol. 47. 6, 761–5

Statement of US Bishops, 'Putting Children and Families First', 14 November 1991, reprinted in *Origins*, 28 November 1991, Vol. 21. 25, 399

Books

Sidney Callahan, *In Good Conscience: Reason and Emotion in Moral Decision Making*, San Francisco 1991

Robert Coles, *The Spiritual Life of Children*, Boston 1990

Mihaly Csikszentmihalyi, *Flow: The Psychology of Optimal Experience*, New York 1990

Howard Gardner, *The Mind's New Science: A History of the Cognitive Revolution*, New York 1987

Adolf Grunbaum, *Validation in the Clinical Theory of Psychoanalysis: A Study in the Philosophy of Psychoanalysis*, New York 1993

Lynn Hoffman, *Foundations of Family Therapy: A Conceptual Framework for Systems Change*, New York 1981

Carroll E. Izard, *The Psychology of Emotions*, New York 1991

Michael J. Mahoney, *Human Change Processes: The Scientific Foundations of Psychotherapy*, New York 1991

Bill Moyers, *Healing and The Mind*, New York 1993

Parenting Across the Life Span: Biosocial Dimensions, ed. Jane B. Lancaster, Jeanne Altmann, Alice S. Rossi and Lonnie R. Sherrod, New York 1987

Person Schemas and Maladaptive Interpersonal Pattens, ed. Mardi J. Horowitz, Chicago 1991

Steven Pinker, *The Language Instinct: How the Mind Creates Language*, New York 1994

Rebuilding the Nest: A New Commitment to the American Family, ed. David Blankenhorn, Steven Bayme and Jean Bethke Elshtain, Milwaukee, WI 1990

Ana-Maria Rizzuto, *The Birth of The Living God: A Psychoanalytic Study*, Chicago 1979
Daniel N. Stern, *The Interpersonal World of the Infant: A View from Psychoanalysis and Developmental Psychology*, New York 1985
E. O. Wilson, *Sociobiology: The New Synthesis*, Cambridge, MA 1975
D. W. Winnicott, *Playing and Reality*, London 1971

Change in the Family and the Challenges of Contemporary Culture

Giorgio Campanini

In the eyes of a church which shares the joys and hopes of humankind (*Gaudium et spes* 1), every change in social reality is at the same time a stimulus and a call. However, in no sphere has it been possible to verify so precisely the close connection between the proclamation of salvation and cultural dynamics as in that of the family, given that the family is both a sociological context and a theological context, since it is founded on a sacrament which is both a human reality and the mystery of salvation. In this sense the changes which have taken place in family relationships cannot fail to represent a serious issue for theological reflection as well.

On that basis, I shall offer some reflections on change in the family and the questions that this raises for Christian awareness which – taking up Arnold Toynbee's well-known theory on the origins of civilization – can be defined as challenge and response. Any cultural change is also a challenge to the churches and in turn always implies the courage to make an adequate response.

The meaning of sexuality

The first and perhaps most radical 'challenge' relates to the general view of sexuality. In the Christian tradition, this has always been thought of as a strong experience: the fact that already in the Jewish tradition and even more in the Christian tradition, sexual disorder has been considered an offence against both human beings and God, attests the presence of this strong vision of the sexual. It is centred, positively, on what is the normal typical foundation of Christian sexual ethics, namely the perception of marriage as the sole place in which it is possible to exercise responsibly a sexuality willed by God and blessed by God. However, in regular currents of contemporary culture sexuality seems to have lost its originally strong sense and to have acquired a weak sense, to the point of trivialization: the dimension of sexual pleasure is emphasized and – in extreme cases – absolutized, and above all isolated from its natural context, namely marriage.

Contrary to the tendency to split sexuality, marriage and family, it is important to provide a new basis, taking account of the new insights of the social sciences into sexuality, a deeper and more authentic understanding of sexuality, renewing its original bond with marriage and making the relationship between the couple, including its sexual dimension but not seeing that as the exclusive feature, a basic element in a relationality open to the gift of life. In a culture like ours today, which is dominated by a tendency towards separation, it is important to recover a profound sense of unity. If this is done, marriage will take on its full symbolic significance by uniting some aspects (interpersonal relations, sexual love, openness to procreation) which the modern culture of sexuality threatens to divide.

The institution put in question

The Christian tradition has been put in question in contemporary culture from another aspect, namely in connection with the relationship between the couple and the institution of marriage. That the love between man and woman, including its dimension of openness to life, should *intrinsically* be given a public dimension seemed abundantly clear to the cultures of the past, as it does to many other cultures which still exist in today's world. These have always made a clear distinction between transitory and promiscuous sexual unions and those which are stable and are given social legitimation through marriage, in its various forms and expressions. However, in a culture like that of the West, which is increasingly being privatized, the distinction between *de facto* relations and those which have and seek a public dimension is becoming blurred, and this is becoming particularly evident in the institution of marriage.

In the presence of these markedly privatistic tendencies, rather than defending the institution of marriage abstractly, or solely at a legal level, it is important to recover its profound significance as the natural projection of the feeling of love and as an innate stimulus towards manifesting this love and having it recognized by the community. The institution of 'banns of marriage' attests this deep wish to communicate what had originally been kept secret and manifests the natural tendency of love to communicate itself and have itself recognized by others. Marriage as an institution is simply the historical context of this concern for recognition: 'free love', voluntary unions, the various precarious forms of relationship between the sexes, do not express with such force this profound urge which authentic love has for recognition by society. The law limits itself to receiving and authenticating this awareness.

The challenge of duration

The third challenge – which is relatively new in history – is that of duration. Marriage in the past was eroded by the brevity of life: marriage today tends to be long, and in advanced industrialized societies, projections of its duration are now approaching fifty years. This not only offers new opportunities but also new problems for couples, who are called on to achieve a deep communion in life not only during the period of falling in love, the first experiences of life together or the period during which their children are being educated, but also in full maturity and the autumn of life. This is the first time that this has happened in history, and it is not surprising that consistent percentages of married couples fail to overcome the challenge of long marriages.

However, in this context, too, the family is called on to maintain its fidelity and renew it over time through the relationship between couples, and also in the exercise of a parental function which is internally creative and open to the future.

From this perspective, the prolongation of marriage in time represents a new opportunity for the modern couple to undertake to express all its potentialities. Marriage can offer a horizon of stability and fidelity in a context in which everything changes, but in which the inevitable disorientation brought about by social change can be overcome through a capacity constantly to enrich everyday life with meaning, even when it seems to get more grey. Divorce adds change to change: fidelity introduces the necessary corrective of emotional and affective stability within the process of change which is essential for both the older and the younger generation.

'Responsibility' under discussion

Western culture has developed through the principle of responsibility, which in turn is bound up with the emerging values of freedom, autonomy and the spirit of initiative. The irruption of the principle of responsibility into the sphere of the family has produced the two great revolutions of everyday life which are represented on the one hand by the affirmation of the legal principle of the free choice of the spouse (matrimonial responsibility) and on the other by the adoption of the criterion of relating procreative behaviour to the dimension of the family, to its educative and its economic capacity (procreative responsibility).

However, if pushed to extremes, the principle of responsibility ends up by destroying itself: it risks making marriage in fact impossible by loading it with too much responsibility, encouraging a preference for unions in which responsibility is less markedly felt (*de facto* unions). At the same time the application of the principle of responsibility to the gift of life loads it with so many conditions as to make it in fact impracticable (the demographic decline typical of many economically advanced Western countries seems symbolic from this perspective).

The question is therefore how to rediscover a principle of responsibility which is open and positive, which does not exclude the possiblity of risk and adventure; as attitudes on the part of couples which put them in charge not only of their own individual destiny but also of the future of the community, thus overcoming a narrowly privatistic view of life.

The family and the new femininity

No less serious is the challenge which the family faces from the emergence of a new image of femininity. The legal parity of man and woman achieved in many countries of the world is accompanied by a constant growth in the level of female culture and the affirmation of an industrial society in which, now that physical strength has become marginal, the first and traditional historical discriminating factor between men and women has ceased to exist. At the same time, the great prolongation of middle life and the change in procreative styles have led to the overcoming of the traditional identification of femininity with the maternal role: in industrial societies, motherhood is still an important reality in the life of the majority of women, but it no longer represents the sole centre.

To respond to the challenge of the new femininity without obscuring the riches which derive from the differentiation rather than the homologization of the sexes, what is needed is a general rebalancing in the life of the couple of the traditional male and female tasks, including those relating to education and domesticity. If there is not to be a crisis in the family, the 'exit' of the wife from the home has to be matched by at least a partial 'return' of the husband, with a view to achieving a fairer relationship between the sexes and a division of tasks and responsibilities corresponding to the new context in which the husband and wife now find themselves. The future of the family to a great extent depends on its capacity to pass from a relationship based on subordination to one based on reciprocity.

The 'new citizenship' of the family

The last challenge which contemporary culture poses to the family is that of the 'new citizenship', or the new relationship with society to which it is called by the prevailing cultural dynamic. The process of the privatization of the Western family is revealing all its limitations, and the family, imprisoned in its solitude, runs the risk of being relegated to the sphere of insignificance. Furthermore, the weighty intrusion into family life of the mass media, which convey a vision that is often hedonistic and orientated on consumption, risks distorting the physiognomy of the family and relegating it to the role of a mere appendix to the productive system and the consumer society.

In the face of the danger of the expropriation of the family and its reduction to a mere sounding-board for a consumer society, it seems necessary to recover a different and fairer relationship with society. The 'new citizenship of the family' represents an awareness of the need for it once again to enter into dialogue with public and indeed social political powers: not only in the name of the values of which it is the vehicle, and which remain basic to any society (from solidarity to the capacity for mediating in and overcoming conflicts), but also in view of breakdowns that are not only personal but also social, which may and in fact do derive from the crisis of the family or even from its desegregation (with costs which are also economic and not just human, and of which all advanced industrial societies are now forced to take account.

Confronting change

The cultural processes which involve the contemporary family – and which have been reduced to the general category of 'challenge' – can all be related to the overall framework sketched out above. The tendency to avoid marriage typical of many members of the new generations, the attempt to promote (and in part to legitimize) families which are not based on institutions, the difficulty of achieving stability in the family, the tendency for conflict between husband and wife, the thrust towards the privatization (and often towards the social marginalization) of the family are the overall framework in which the reality of the family is situated in this phase of the century.

Confronted with this scenario, sociology as such does not have recipes to offer, but can only try to describe or at most to understand. However, not even this approach can completely avoid making a value judgment well beyond the concrete forms of the living and organizing of family life, on its roots in the profound nature of man and woman. The historical failure of the different alternatives to the family and the parallel observation of the negative effects of its crisis enable us to conclude that the 'formal family' orientated on stability and based on marriage is and remains the foundation of any just society. No better future can be constructed that leaves aside this sphere of life which is irreplacable for men and women, above all for those who were coming together for the first time and need a structure which will support them on the way to the achievement of full personal maturity.

Translated by John Bowden

Bibliography

G. Agostinucci and G. Campanini, *La questione femminile – Chiesa e storia*, Casale Monferrato 1989
Angelli Foundation, *Famiglia, figli, società in Europa*, Turin 1991
R.N. Anshen (ed.), *The Family, Its Function and Destiny*, New York 1959
P. Ariès, *L'enfant et la vie familiale sous l'ancien Régime*, Paris 1968
M. Barbagli, *Provando e riprovando — Famiglia e divorzio in Italia e in altri paesi occidentali*, Bologna 1990
P. and P.L. Berger, *The War over the Family*, London 1983
G. Campanini, *Realtà e problemi della famiglia contemporanea*, Milan 1989
— (ed.)., *Le stagioni della famiglia*, Milan 1994
P. Donti, *La cittadinanza societaria*, Bari and Rome 1993
— , 'Famiglia: Pubblico/Privato', in *Dizionario delle idee politiche*, ed. E. Berti and G. Campanini, Rome 1993
H. Jonas, *Das Prinzip Verantwortung*, 1990
G. Lévi-Strauss, *Les structures élémentaires de la parenté*, Paris 1969

Faith, Feminism and the Family
Linda Woodhead

Introduction

Feminism is not notorious for championing the family. Indeed, amongst the barrage of attacks on the family which have been launched since the mid 1960s, the feminist critique stands out as one of the most powerful. Central in several of the foundational works of 'second phase' feminism, this critique remains important in many of the varied forms of feminist thought which have arisen since.[1]

The feminist critique of the family tends to work on two levels. At the first level, it criticizes the family for its key place in a patriarchal society, seeing it as the intimate environment in which unequal and destructive relations between the sexes trap the current generation and shape the next. At an even more fundamental level, feminism opposes any fixed form of association which dictates the ways in which women and men organize their lives and live out their relationships. Feminists generally maintain that every woman should have the right to live in intimate association with whomever she chooses – whether on her own, as a single mother, in partnership with another man or woman, or in some freely-chosen form of experimental community.

In contrast to feminism throughout the course of its long history Christianity has been much readier to champion the family. Even during periods when the prestige of celibacy was at its highest, the church did not condemn the family. At its most negative, the church has defended family life as one possible form of Christian life. At its most positive, it has celebrated family life as the divinely ordained norm for all Christians. The family, according to Christian belief, is part of the order of God's creation. It has one foot in paradise, being ordained by God 'from the beginning', and another in the fallen order, being part of God's gracious ordinance for that order. Only in the eschatological order is the family's existence and validity in doubt,[2] and as eschatological belief has faded in the modern period, Christianity's high evaluation of the family has, if anything, increased. Whilst Protestants would once reproach Catholics for their denigration of the family, both denominations seem now to speak as one in their support for the family.

Has the family thus become the rock on which all attempts to find some rapprochement between Christianity and feminism must inevitably founder? Many feminists, and perhaps some Christians, believe this to be the case. In what follows, I wish to question this pessimistic acceptance of a stalemate, and to point out a possible way round the impasse. Its starting point is one of the key affirmations of feminist thought – the affirmation of the importance of the body, of the essentially embodied nature of human existence. What I hope to show is that if this is taken seriously and followed where it logically leads, it gives rise to a 'high doctrine' of the family, and provides an independent but complementary justification for Christianity's support of the family. The justification is one which can appeal to non-Christians as well as Christians, and is in that sense 'natural'.

Feminism, Christianity and the body

Feminists are not the first nor the only thinkers to affirm the importance of the body, but the feminist reaffirmation of the essential embodiedness of human beings has been powerful and timely, and has had a particular relevance to Christianity.

Feminism's acknowledgement of the importance of the body arose out of a wider enterprise: the exploration of patriarchal stereotypes of women and resistance to those stereotypes. One of the foundational insights of feminist thought was that these stereotypes typically cast the female in dualistic opposition to the male, and that the most influential of these dualistic oppositions is that between that the male as spiritual and the female as embodied or between the male as cultural and the female as natural. The spirit/body dualism is common in much pre-modern thought and is plausibly seen as an important part of the Christian inheritance, whilst the culture/nature dualism is viewed as its more modern manifestation.[3]

Having exposed the identification of women with the body, feminism sought not to overturn it by claiming that women are more spiritual than men, nor even to level it by claiming that they are equally spiritual. Rather, in a more far-reaching and subversive move, feminism accepted the identification of women with the body and amplified it into the wider affirmation of the essential embodiedness of all women and (in most varieties of feminism) of all men. Feminism made the plausible claim that women, having always been viewed in bodily terms, have found it much easier than men to accept their embodiedness and live in truthful acceptance of it. Men, deluded into thinking of themselves as spiritual beings, have been condemned to live in an unhappy state of war with the body and with nature, engaged always in the impossible and destructive struggle to subdue and conquer them.

The feminist critique of the spiritualization of the human (or at least the male) has identified Christianity as a key culprit in the whole process. Whilst some feminists believe that the spirit/body, male-female dualism is so basic to Christianity that rejection of it means the rejection of Christianity, a much better case can be made for saying that the feminist critique of these oppositions does not destroy Christianity but recalls it to its own true understanding of what it is to be human, male and female. It recalls Christianity to a more thoroughgoing acceptance of many of its central credal beliefs: that the material world was created by God and was 'good'; that the spirit is the giver of life, bound up with the creation, not an alien element trapped within it; that God took human flesh, and was raised in the same form; that humans are created as embodied creatures, destroyed as embodied creatures, and live again in the resurrection life as embodied creatures. Christianity and feminism should be allies, not enemies, in their affirmation of the importance of the body.

The body and the family: a natural defence of the family

Feminism's acknowledgment of the inevitably embodied nature of human existence carries with it many important implications, and much feminist thought is devoted to spelling out what these might be. The implication on which I want to dwell is, however, one that is rarely if ever acknowledged. It is that bodily relatedness, the 'blood tie', is a uniquely important form of relation. If we really believe that bodies matter, and are prepared to follow this insight where it takes us, we cannot help but acknowledge that the fact that a child is produced by the bodily union of its mother and father, that the mother carries it in her body for nine months, that the child usually shares many of its parent's bodily features and bears their genetic inheritance, is of enormous significance and provides a uniquely firm foundation for a relationship of love.

The strength of the love between those who are bound by the blood tie flows directly from the nature of that tie. Because we are embodied creatures and because a child or sibling is, in the words of a common phrase, 'one's own flesh and blood', we do not clearly separate our own existence from theirs. So we love them not with a selfless love, but with self-love – the most constant and unfailing of all the loves.[4] Moreover, the recognition that a child or sibling is 'my own flesh and blood' is a recognition of their fundamental identity and equality with oneself. Because our sinful refusal to recognize this equality with others is so often the ground of our refusal to love them. The fact one has an undeniable identity with those close relatives makes one's love for them that much more firmly rooted.

So the acknowledgment of the importance of the body leads to the acknowledgment that there is a unique bond between those related by blood or, as we might say, related by body. Given the importance of this bond, it would be strange if society were not organized to take account of it. It would, in other words, be strange if the family did not exist, for at its minimum the family is simply that social unit composed of parents and their offspring, at its maximum the wider group who are related by blood ties. The existence of family units of greater or smaller size in almost all human cultures of which we have knowledge is surely the clearest indication we have of the near universal recognition of the importance of bodily relatedness.[5]

Feminist resistance to the family

If, as I have been arguing, a recognition of the essentially embodied nature of human existence should lead to a recognition of the importance of the family, it seems strange that feminism can in one breath affirm the importance of the body and deny that of the family. The most important reason for this inconsistency is, it seems, feminism's often uncritical acceptance of the typically modern assumption that society has no natural foundations, but is purely cultural, purely the product of human agency. In the succinct formulation of Roberto Unger: society is an artefact.[6] As such, society is infinitely malleable. The limits of its possible configurations are nothing but the limits of human imagination and ingenuity. Tied to the equally strong modern belief in progress, this view of society gives birth to the hope that there is always a better arrangement waiting around the corner and that all present and past forms of social organization have a merely provisional validity – the family being no exception.

It is, however, inconsistent to accept the importance of the body and at the same time to adopt without reservation the modern constructivist, technological attitude. For in acknowledging the importance of the body one acknowledges that some things are natural, not created; given, not made. As Oliver O'Donovan puts it:

> The relation of human beings to their own bodies, we might say, is the last frontier of nature. However much we may surround ourselves with our artefacts, banish every bird from the sky and every fish from the river . . . however blind we may become to the givenness of the natural order on which our culture is erected, nevertheless, when we take off our clothes to have a bath, we confront something as natural, as given, as completely non-artefactual as anything in the universe: we confront our own bodily existence.[7]

The desire to reject the family, as much as the desire to reject the body, springs from a failure to acknowledge that there are things we have not created but which we must nonetheless respect. Ecological thought is one counter-current in modernity which seeks to recall us to this old truth, and feminist thought (especially 'eco-feminism') is increasingly sympathetic to this message.[8] Yet its implications for social organization, especially where the family is concerned, continue to be largely ignored.

Not all feminist resistance to the family, however, depends on an uncritical adoption of the modern technological spirit and a failure to see that this contradicts belief in the importance of the body. Some feminists resist the family, not because they deny that the body and bodily relatedness matter, but because they deny that they matter *enough* to form the basis for social arrangements. According to such thinkers, the blood tie is just one sort of bond between humans and is much less important than, say, freely-chosen emotional bond. In support of this, it is pointed out, first, that there are many strong human bonds which are not based on blood – perhaps most notably the married relationship and the adoptive relationship; and second, that blood ties do not seem in themselves to be enough to guarantee love or even respect – as the case of the dysfunctional or even abusive family shows.

Whilst there is no doubt that these examples prove that lasting and loving bonds do not necessarily depend upon bodily relatedness, it is not at all clear that they disprove the claim that bodily relatedness is nevertheless the strongest foundation for human relationships. Even though we can happily admit that the love found in married and adoptive relationships can be as strong and true and lasting as any other love, it would be hard to deny that both are more fragile than the love between natural child and parent. Nor can it be denied that abuse within families is more commonly perpetrated by, for example, a husband on a wife or a stepfather on a stepdaughter than by a blood relative. It is rarest of all between those bound by the strongest of bodily ties: a mother and her son or daughter.

Against the feminist dismissal of the importance of the physical relationship, it is also important to point out that this bond has priority over other sorts of human bond in that it furnishes the model and the ideal for them, not they for it. Thus in the case of adoption, adoptive parents may say to their child, quite truthfully, 'we love you as our own child', or even 'you are our own child', and it would be a misunderstanding for the child to want more. But a natural parent would never say, 'I love you as an adopted child'. In a similar way the physical bond is used as a quarry for talk and thought where marriage is concerned. The most privileged way of speaking of marriage in the Bible and the Christian tradition is thus as the cleaving together of a man and a woman to become 'one flesh' (Gen. 2.24; Matt. 19.5–6; Mark 10.8; I Cor. 16.6; Eph. 5.31).[9] To argue that this is just a metaphor is to forget that metaphors are usually employed because they are strong enough to carry the weight assigned to them. The language of 'one flesh' opens our eyes to some essential aspects of the marriage relationship – for example, to the intimate physical union which occurs in sexual intercourse between a man and a woman and to the way in which children bind their parents together, physically relating them to one another.[10] Even more importantly, this language tells us that marriage should be a bond as strong as the blood tie – that is to say, the strongest of all bonds.

The feminist assertion that the physical bond is a weaker bond than other human bonds is therefore hard to sustain. It does, however, contain one important insight: that human beings are not mere bodies and that human relationships cannot be reduced to mere physical relatedness. Christianity has often used the language of 'soul' or 'spirit' to signal this truth, but feminism is right to point out that such language too often lends itself to a dualistic view of human existence. Feminism prefers to speak of human beings as 'cultural' as well as 'natural', thereby acknowledging that we do not just respond passively to what is given, but interpret and shape it at both an individual and a collective level. In other words, our bodies are given, but we write on them in different ways, and we write with them in different ways. What the language of 'culture' fails to convey, however, is that these ways may be godly or ungodly. We can live spiritual or we can live fleshly lives, we can save or we can lose our souls.

And it is precisely because we can lose our souls that the physical bond cannot guarantee a lasting and loving relationship. Loving relatedness is not a matter of bodily relatedness alone; the latter must deepen into a kinship of feeling, thinking, motivation and concern if it is to mature into love. Nothing, not even the blood tie, can guarantee that one human being will love another, for love is a freely bestowed gift – and as such it may always be withheld. This is why there are dysfunctional families, and the feminist critique of the family has been immensely valuable where it has exposed these dysfunctions, particularly those in which female members of the family become the victims. Yet the fact that human beings can sin, and the fact that forms of social association can be distorted by such sin, is surely a very poor reason for abandoning those forms.

Christian resistance to the family

Some Christians feel as resistant to the family as do feminists, albeit for different reasons. One powerful source of Christian resistance to the family is the belief that *agape*, the love which should lie at the heart of the Christian life, is a spiritual, not a physical love. Beside the supposed disinterestedness and universality of *agape*, those loves which have a bodily basis and the institutions which support them appear inferior and worldly.[11]

But is *agape* really as exclusively 'spiritual' as is claimed? Closer attention to the Bible shows that in fact descriptions of *agape* frequently draw upon the language of physical relationship. This is often true even where divine *agape*, God's *agape* for his creatures, is concerned – as the parable of the prodigal son dramatically demonstrates. Not that the Bible suggests for a moment that we are tied to God by any form of bodily relation: Jesus Christ is the *only*-begotten Son of the Father; we are creatures formed from dust. Yet we are assured that we can become children of God by grace – not by birth but by 'adoption' – 'and if children, then heirs' (Rom. 8.15–17). We can truthfully call God 'Father', 'Abba', because the spirit of the Son has been sent into our hearts (Gal. 4.5–7).

Turning to human *agape*, love of human beings for one another, it is true that Jesus' teaching insists that this love is not to be reserved for members of one's family or even one's race. Yet the implication is not that relationships of bodily connection should be neglected, but rather that one's understanding of the extent of such connection should be widened. As Paul makes clear, all those who are baptized are baptized into the body of Christ, they become members of the one body; *agape* should flow from recognition of this bodily relatedness (e.g. I Cor. 12.12–27; Rom. 12.4–6). And although Paul speaks of human *agape* primarily as the love which binds Christians to one another, this does not mean that it should not be shown to those outside the church for, as the parable of the sheep and the goats shows, it is never easy to be sure where Christ's body begins and ends: 'As you did it to the least of my family, you did it to me' (Matt. 25.40).[12]

Though the nature of *agape* is therefore not such as to provide Christians with a reason for spurning bodily relatedness and resisting the family, it does provide good grounds for resisting 'family worship', the tendency to treat the domestic unit as the only sphere of authentic existence and moral responsibility.[13] As has been mentioned, to attribute this sort of ultimacy to the family is to ignore its provisionality within the perspective of the eschatological and the eternal. It is also to forget that in this age, the age before the eschaton, there are 'orders of creation' which are just as important as the family: most notably the polity and the church. Our duties as worshippers and citizens are just as important as those as family members, and it is vital that these duties constantly check one another. Ferdinand Mount has shown convincingly that the family can serve as an important check on the power of the state.[14] What he fails to mention is that conversely, church and the state serve as important checks on the family, preventing its shrinkage to an introverted and solipsistic unit.

Conclusion

The fact that there is today a widespread and growing hostility to the family should not surprise us. Many of the most powerful currents of modernity oppose the family. The technological spirit which wishes to manipulate and change everything, including social arrangements, resists it. The libertarian temper which wishes to be bound by nothing that is not freely and 'authentically' chosen resists it. The general refusal to accept that we live in a world which is given and natural as well as chosen and cultural/historical resists it. The still pervasive belief in progress and the redundancy of past forms resists it. And the spiritualizing and idealizing temper of the times which understands the authentically human not in terms of the body but in terms of the human spirit resists it.

Christianity and feminism both display ambiguous attitudes to modernity. On the one hand they both question and resist many of modernity's most cherished convictions. On the other, they both accept a great deal of the modern ethos, often oblivious to how much it compromises their own foundational beliefs. As this article has tried to show, feminism has been enormously helpful to Christianity in recalling it to a belief in the importance of the bodily and in showing how much it had compromised itself by collaborating with modernity's spiritualization of the human. As this article has also tried to show, Christianity may now be in a position to return the favour by showing feminism that its uncritical acceptance of some key aspects of the modern ethos has prevented it from acknowledging the importance of the family. In doing so, Christianity could help feminism come to a full acceptance of the implications of its belief in the importance of the body for the first time. No less significant, it could help reassure the millions of women who are sustained and fulfilled through love of husband and children that there really is no reason why they should continue to feel traitors to the feminist cause.[15]

Notes

1. Several of the feminists whose books appeared in the late 1960s and early 1970s referred to their work as a 'second phase' of feminism, contrasting it with the 'first wave' which, focussed on winning the vote for women, was made redundant by that victory (though to my mind it is actually the publication of Simone de Beauvoir's *Le Deuxième Sexe* in 1949 which marks the start of a second phase of feminism). Of the most prominent second-phase feminists, Kate Millett, Germaine Greer and Shulamith Firestone were the most outspoken critics of the family. For an account of post-1960s attacks on the family, including those by feminists, see R. Fletcher, *The Abolitionists: The Family and Marriage under Attack*, London 1988, and B. Berger and P. L. Berger, *The War over the Family: Capturing the Middle Ground*, London 1983.

2. Jesus' words 'in the resurrection they neither marry nor are given in marriage' (Matt. 22.30) were influential for later Christian thought about the eschaton.

3. Simone de Beauvoir's *Le Deuxième Sexe* highlighted the way in which woman is treated as 'Other', and in particular as 'Nature' as opposed to transcendant Spirit. Simone de Beauvoir, *The Second Sex*, London 1968, 1-29, 171-229. On the nature-culture dualism and women see the influential essay by S. B. Ortner, 'Is Female to Male as Nature is to Culture?', M. Z. Rosaldo and L. Lampere (eds.) *Woman, Culture and Society*, Berkeley, Ca.

4. According to Augustine, Jesus himself recognized the primacy of self-love in commanding 'you shall love your neighbour as yourself', *De Doctrina Christiana* I,22.

5. On the ubiquity of the family see R. Fletcher, *The Shaking of the Foundations: Family and Society*, London 1988; and F. Mount, *The Subversive Family*, London 1982.

6. See Robin W. Lovin and Michael J. Perry (eds), *Critique and Construction: A Symposium on Roberto Unger's Politics*, Cambridge 1990.

7. O. O'Donovan, *Begotten or Made?*, Oxford 1984,5.

8. See, for example, S. Griffin, *Woman and Nature*, New York 1978; Anne Primavesis, *Apocalypse to Genesis*, Tunbridge Wells 1991.

9. 'Flesh' in the Bible does not always mean simply the bodily aspect of a person but, as here, may refer to the whole human person.

10. In the latter context it is interesting to recall Edward Westermarck's concluding remarks in *The History of Human Marriage*: 'It is originally for the benefit of the young that male and female continue to live together. We may therefore say that marriage is rooted in the family rather than the family in marriage.' Quoted by Fletcher, *The Shaking of the Foundations* (n.5), 32.

11. I have discussed this interpretation of *agape* and the problems which it raises at greater length in 'Love and Justice', *Studies in Christian Ethics* 5.1, 1993, 44–61.

12. It should not be forgotten that traditional Christian thought saw human beings as physically related to one another through Adam as well as through Christ. Thus Augustine and other Christian commentators explain Eve's creation out of the rib of Adam in these terms: 'Therefore, God created one sole individual, not that he was meant to remain alone deprived of human companionship, but in order that the unity of society and the bond of harmony might mean more to man, since men were united not only by the likeness of nature, but also by the affection of kinship. God did not even wish to create the woman who was to be mated with man in the same way that he created man, but, rather, out of him, in order that the whole human race might be derived entirely from one single individual'. Augustine, *City of God*, XII, 22.

13. This idolatrous attitude to the family is one which tends to have more devastating consequences for women's lives than for men's. See Betty Friedan's critique of post-war American domesticity and its effects on women in *The Feminine Mystique*, New York 1963.

14. See Mount, *Subversive Family*, (n.5).

15. Several of the contributors to S. Wilkinson and C. Kittinger (eds.). *Heterosexuality*, London 1993 admit honestly to this feeling, one commenting that 'having a good husband seems to be many feminists' well-guarded secret' (34).

The Family in the 'Peripheral World'

Enrique Dussel

What is called Western culture (European-North American) is often identified with what is 'universally' Christian as such. So the *European* family is identified with what is seen as being the *Christian* family. The 'usual' theological treatment of the subject begins with a study of the family in the Old and New Testaments, goes on to analyse it in Roman and mediaeval culture, and ends with an examination of it in modern Europe.[1] In this way, judgments are passed on contemporary change in late capitalist societies. No account is taken of the fact that this viewpoint – historically and systematically – is *exclusively* European and is valid today for some twelve per cent of the world's population.[2]

So this article has to deal with the question of the family as it affects the major part of humanity. The question is so closely linked to daily life that it is not surprising that the Special Assembly of the Synod of Bishops for Africa, which ended in Rome on 8 May 1994, made marriage and the family one of the central issues in its debates, and that it was the one that aroused the strongest feelings. Mgr Monsengwo, speaking of the 'unity and indissolubility of marriage', indicated that this was not opposed to the question of polygamy (one form of matrimonial 'unity') or divorce (which can come about as an exception in some cases of separation, contradicting a rigorist and universal view of indissolubility). This led to a request for a Pontifical Commission to study the '*African* Catholic code of marriage'. Subjects requiring study would be the 'joint or extended' family, gradual marriage, the difference between marriage *ratum* and *consummatum*, the levirate law, rituals enriched by local customs, and so on.[3] As can be seen, these are not questions 'normally' analysed in theological treatises on the family.

I. The problem of the 'Christian' family: revelation and institutionalization

The 'nuclear family', understood as consisting exclusively of mother/father and daughters/sons,[4] has become generalized in the 'central' countries of the World System[5] since the end of the Second World War,[6] and is tending to predominate in the conurbations of the 'periphery', owing in both cases mainly to the wage structure (earned generally by the father, also often by the mother, which enables the nuclear family to enjoy economic autonomy), to the mobility required by capitalist business, and to pensions and social security (which now allow autonomy to the 'third age').[7] The extended family provided the means of biological survival, of security and psychological, cultural and religious apprenticeship, and, furthermore, of economic inheritance, which means that it was indispensable until a few decades ago – and that we have still not appreciated the values we have lost with its disappearance.

In the same way, the stable (I do not say 'indissoluble') pair bond (I do not say 'married couple') of '*one* woman/*one* man' (monoandric, monogamous), although empirically present in all countries of the world – since the evolutionary hypothesis became unsustainable some time ago – ,[8] is very far from being institutionally exclusive and indissoluble. There is an immense, very complex and highly differentiated variety of *family* relationships that can be established between men/women, their mothers/fathers (grandmothers/grandfathers), their sisters/brothers (aunts/uncles), their direct daughters/sons and those of their sisters/brothers and of their aunts/uncles (cousins in varying degrees); if one goes farther and takes great-grandparents (fourth generation) and great-great-grandparents (fifth generation) into account, family or clan (totemic or not) relationships can be built up extending to several hundred or even thousand persons.[9] All these members of the extended family have established functions within it and well defined types of 'belonging' (rights and duties) 'sacredly' carried out (since social customs are generally identified with religious symbols, myths and rites, surrounding the veneration and memory of the totem or 'ancestors'). Eboussi Boulanga has described all this beautifully and profoundly from an ontological and religious standpoint in his magnificent book *La crise du Muntu*:

> What the *origin* preserves in itself is real [sacred]. What the *origin* preserves in itself as provenance under the form of hierarchy or genealogy is real [sacred]. What the *origin* preserves in itself as

destination under the form of reintegration is real [sacred].[10] . . . The succession of generations, the place of individuals [in the family], are determined and evaluated by the greater or lesser distance that separates them from the origin or from the one who actualizes this by representing it . . . Authenticity is given only by this permanent authorization of the origin, by this actuality of the originating power.[11]

The extended family is the very nucleus of real existence, of the religious symbolizing of existence, of the rhythm of life, of nature, of dance. This is why we cannot simplify the question of the family and speak only of the modern family and the traditional family.[12]

But – and this is my main point – there is far more reason not to confuse the said modern family with the 'Christian' family as such.[13] In the first place, there is no *perfect* 'Christian' family that has been revealed in 'this' specific manner. What we have are *revealed ethical criteria and principles*[14] which 'work' *within* 'any' possible culture, making its existing structures (whatever they may be, including polyandry or polygamy, etc.) progress toward a situation in which interpersonal ethical relationships (of whatever type) among *all family members* (in their possible and multiple horizontal *relationships* of brother/sisterhood, pairing [love, fidelity, etc.], or vertical relationships of maternity, paternity, son/daughterhood, grandparents to grandchildren, etc.) are superseded, or grow, or mature. In the New Testament, Jesus *did not reveal a specific socio-historical type of family structure*, since, for example, he did not put forward an indissolubility without exceptions, but admitted that in the past a wife could be put away by her husband.[15] Therefore, to say in an abstract or non space/time-situated fashion that simultaneous polygamy is 'contrary to Christian law'[16] is profoundly ambiguous (and in a way false). It was not so in the Old Testament, and St Augustine allowed polygamy for the purposes of procreation.[17] Once the European-mediaeval family structure, that of Christendom (which is not Christianity),[18] was *identified* with the 'Christian' family as such, any other historical type of family structure was judged to be contrary to the structure of the *revealed Christian* family. But, once again, as the 'rule' by which the Christian morality of a Christian family institution in Latin America, Africa or Asia was measured was not *revealed criteria and principles* but the actual historical structure of the European-modern family already established in the fifteenth century, the negative judgment made of family organization in the Peripheral World was nothing other than the effect of a deforming and anti-Christian Eurocentrism, offensive to the dignity of other cultures and objectively dominating – which is still more or less the criterion in force today.

II. The European-missionary expansion and sexual violence of Christians in America

The experience of the Renaissance was carried on in Spain as the beginning of the modern age, that is, as the start, in 1492, of the expansion and installation of the first 'World System'.[19] The theme of the family was a constituent of the process of conquest and colonization, which went hand-in-hand with that of evangelization,[20] being, unfortunately, part of the process of not recognizing the otherness of others.[21]

It is all too well known that the indigenous American populations were the first to suffer the de-structurizing impact on the continent's age-old family, whose cultural validity was rigidly accepted by each nation.[22] The arrival of the white outsiders brought about a 'relaxation' of previous native customs and produced chaos in the indigenous family structure. Spanish and Portuguese men (warriors at first and then colonizers) killed native men in the military violence of the conquest and 'went to bed' with ('lived with', they said in the sixteenth century) Indian women: 'La Malinche' (Cortes' mistress) became the symbol of the mother-concubine of mixed race.[23] *Mestizos* are themselves sons/daughters without a father, or without a 'normal' family – most children do not have a legally (let alone ecclesially) constituted family in Latin America: in Panama seventy per cent of children are born out of wedlock.[24] As an institution effectively started with the conquest and colonization, the family situation obtaining in Latin America shows the following variants: 1. the monogamous family, presented as the Christian 'ideal'; 2. marriage by social consent, not legally celebrated; 3. the family in which the husband in effect practises bigamy (with a second wife 'from the people', a 'Margarita' from the slums, who then becomes the prostitute 'Margo' in the tango of the same name), which *machismo* makes even white wives tolerate; 4. the mother with children by different fathers (the commonest form), or the father without a family who seeks relations with women outside any form of marriage. The church always required the Indians, colonial society, rural or urban, to observe strict, 'ideal' monogamy, but it never clearly appreciated the real customs of violence brought in by the process of conquest itself (and later consecrated by evangelization): the way the indigenous population was organized (by the system of urban or rural 'reductions'), the imposition of Hispanic machismo on the dominated (conquered) indigenous family, the inculcation of habits of erotic oppression (product of military, economic or political hegemony),[25] the fragility of poor women faced with the power of money, the conditions of poverty that made it impossible for men 'of the people' to build a 'normal' family, and so on. That is, the church never faced up to reality so that it might adopt pastoral measures to deal with an objectively observed situation. It always hid the reality behind the ideal family – which did not exist. The present situation is horrifying in every sense of the word.

The situation of the African-American population of Latin America and the Caribbean has its own peculiar characteristics,[26] since it suffered an even greater destructuration at the hands of the white Christian elites than the Indians. Slaves were frequently forbidden to set up families or contract marriage, or even enter into stable relationships. White men claimed unlimited 'rights' to sexual use of black women. This was actually part of 'business', since it produced new slaves – mere merchandise within the fetishism of slavery accepted in Europe. In the name of this 'Christian civilization', real atrocities have been committed against the family of dominated peoples – a fact too often forgotten. The present situation in the Caribbean is the product of a history of slavery. Today, in general, families are being turned upside-down by the impact of transnational capitalism, urban life and the culture of the mass media.[27] Most black families live in conditions associated with peripheral societies, in which extreme poverty forces a large proportion of the people into marginality – women into concubinage, single motherhood or prostitution, the next generation into being 'street kids', shot as 'rats' by the Brazilian police – the fruit of five hundred years of the modern age.

III. The case of Africa: a failure of understanding through missionary rigorism[28]

Sub-Saharan Africa is where the confrontation between the Christian-missionary world and Bantu civilization is experienced most acutely. It is equally the place where new principles of applying Christian revealed criteria could still be applied in a slow and respectful transformation of family structures that are inter-subjectively valid for a non-European culture, making it possible to work on them from *within* a practice of love of neighbour (the 'face-to-face' responsibility for the Other as other, in all members of the extended family).

We need to start from the ancient doctrine (of Augustine and Thomas Aquinas) of not condemning *a priori* a family institution for not being

European-modern. We need to make a *positive* evaluation of traditional marriage and the extended family (analysing their values of psychological security, economic protection, solidarity, education, etc.), including polygamy (which can be justified in particular cases), African rites and ceremonies, consort compensation, trial marriages, betrothal, child education, broader relationships, and so on. But, at the same time, we need to make plain and put into practice the criteria that should transform these institutions from *within*. This means that we have to define a pastoral approach that respects and responds to African culture.

In Africa, since the Portuguese presence that required the first Bantu king of the colony of Angola to abandon polygamy – choosing one of his wives – missionary failure of understanding (repeated since the nineteenth-century influx of French, English and Italian missionaries) has up to the present produced a situation in which it has been impossible to repeat the creative approach Christians took to Roman Mediterranean culture during the first centuries of Christianity.

IV. The case of Asia: adaptation by the Christian minorities[29]

In Asia, unlike Latin America or Africa, Christian missionary influence has been minimal, but, on the other hand, the impact of transnational capitalism and urban civilization has brought about deep changes in the daily lives of most Asian families. They have involved the nuclear family becoming more and more common in the numerous large cities of Asia – though not in traditional rural areas.

As an exception to this rule, the world of Islam has provided a confrontational frontier with Christianity, from North Africa to the Philippines, for 1400 years.[30] Partly owing to it fundamentalist tendencies, it has resisted the influence of accelerated modernization.

Asia presents a very varied picture.[31] In India,[32] I am told, in 1960 seventy-five per cent of women were opposed to the 'joint family', although in practice the same proportion of familes practised its customs (embracing up to five generations) in the villages in rural areas, where most of the population of India live.[33] Patriarchalism is highly accentuated, buttressed by the caste system. Women are often seriously oppressed. Now the development of capitalism in India, the increasing move to the cities and the mass culture of radio, television and cinema are imposing the nuclear family as elsewhere. But Christians are having little or no effect on this development.[34]

In China, the extended family acquired its traditional structure, deeply influenced by Confucianism, in the Tang Dynasty (618–907 CE).[35] In 1907 the Empire organized a commission to study the family. In 1931 a new Family Code was promulgated in the Republic. But it was the Communist Revolution that produced a deep change in family organization.[36] It was not missionary Christianity but the revolution that imposed the nuclear family in the cities.[37] In the rural areas, however, where most the the population still live, extended family structures still survive, in weakened form, but still following traditional patterns.

Many other cases could be studied, but space does not permit.[38]

V. Is it too late to learn something from the many types of family existing in the Peripheral World?

We hear a lot of talk about the tropical forests and their genetic potential – vegetable, animal and even human. Is it not also the case that the European-North American, modern, secularized, even supposedly Christian, nuclear family has, by and large, completely lost the symbolic, religious sense of 'belonging' to a wider family community to envelop it, assure it and give it meaning? Even though the modern nuclear family has gained many positive values, particularly its sense of individual self-understanding in the areas of guilt-free loving sexual relationships, of freedom of choice in its actions, of personal responsibility for its social commitment, can we, in the final analysis, be so sure that what we have lost in the extended family is less valuable than what has been gained? Or, above all, that many of the positive values that have been lost cannot be recovered through applying a new class of criteria? For example, could not the 'base Christian community' also be a present-day urban (and rural) attempt vitally and specifically to recover the values lost with the extended family – without repeating its mistakes? And, furthermore, if it is this, is it not at the same time the creation of a sort of 'nuclear church'? Would not the pastoral vision of the parish as a 'community', based on nuclear families, have a lot to gain from appropriating the spiritual riches of family structures that still survive in the Peripheral World, not regarding them as museum pieces, but understanding that they represent actual ways in which family experience is lived by the *greater part of humankind*?

Since an *ideal* 'Christian' family does not empirically exist (nor could it exist in a perfect realization), what we need to set about bringing into being is an actual family that is *better* than what we have at present, that *will institutionalize* structures rebuilt on the counter-pretence demands of the gospel – as Søren Kierkegaard analogously and correctly demonstrated, in arguing that the Hegelian claim that the Lutheran 'state' was a 'Christian' state showed only that it was a Christendom, and that its identification with a culture produced the negation of Christianity. The same applies to the 'Christian family'. Evangelizing the existing family structure (of Europe, the United States or the Peripheral World) means starting from 'valid' marriage,[39] from the customs of the family as it exists,[40] from the betrothal, the marriage ceremonies, the upbringing of children, the type of relationship in practice, so as to produce a 'step forward' from within. That is to say, we must not negate customs, but *remodel* them internally; also, it has to be the Christian subjects themselves (fathers, mothers, sons, daughters, grandmothers, etc.) who are charged with creating the new institutions necessary for *Latin American, African or Asian families today* (in their urban, rural and other embodiments) to mature progressively on the basis of the ethical requirements of the gospel.

Translated by Paul Burns

Notes

1. E.g. the article on 'Family' in *Dictionnaire d'Archéologie Chrétienne et Liturgie* V, Paris 1922, 1082–107.
2. Taking the population of Western Europe and the United States in relation to the present world population of 5,000,000.
3. See 'Sínodo Africano', *Misión sin fronteras* 157, Lima 1994, 22.
4. I am leaving aside, as not directly related to my subject, the question of homosexual couples (which function as second generation) and their possible relationship of upbringing with an adopted first generation, which would constitute a very specific form of nuclear family never observed in the past, but also requiring analysis.
5. See Immanuel Wallerstein, *The Modern World-System*, vols. I–III, New York 1974–89.
6. Between the two world wars, grandparents often lived with the nuclear family, even in Europe and the United States.
7. Nevertheless, the vast majority of the world's population are still not insured for any sort of pension in old age, and more than half are without any regular wage. So the means to establish an autonomous nuclear family still do not exist for them, and there seems to be no chance of this being the case in the near future – since the situation is tending to worsen *systematically* through the growing impoverishment of the Peripheral World. In 1960 the richest 20% of humanity enjoyed an income thirty times greater than the poorest 20%; by 1990 this was sixty times more, amounting to 82% of the world's products. See UN Development Programme, *Report on Human Development*, New York 1992.
8. See 'Familie,' *LTK*, IV, 1960, 8–21.

9. Among Hawaians, 'father' means both biological father and paternal and maternal uncles; 'woman' (adult) includes wife and sisters-in-law; and so on with all possible relationships. One of the first norms established in families was exogamy (or exoandry in other cases) together with the incest tabu. Endogamy is exceptional. Polygamy, though, is very widespread in the most diverse cultures, under many forms, and is tied to economic and political power structures – co-existing with the monogamy/ monoandry of most of the population. Polyandry is exceptional, practised under different forms (depending on rights of the first-born, the elevated status of women in some cases, shortage of women for various reasons): see H. Price Peter, *A Study of Polyandry*, The Hague 1963. All this is often ultimately determined by institutionalization of a patriarchal type (the most extensive), either patrilineal or even matrilineal, or matriarchal, either way: see e.g. G. S. Ghurye, *Family and Kin in Indo-European Culture*, London-Bombay 1955; 'Famille', *La Grande Encyclopédie* XVI, Paris n.d.; Harold Christiansen (ed.), *Handbook of Marriage and the Family*, Chicago 1964; Carle Zimmerman, *Family and Civilization*, New York 1974; Robina Quale, *A History of Marriage Systems*, New York 1988.

10. Présence Africaine, Paris 1977, 50.

11. Ibid., 51.

12. 'Traditional' includes the mediaeval or early modern European family, as well as the numerous types of family organization of Latin America, Africa and Asia, all of which clearly implies considerable confusion.

13. The designation 'Christian family' (used in the same way as 'Christian' culture, the 'Christian' state, 'Christian' philosophy, etc.) gives rise to a major misunderstanding. How can a family, a state, a culture or a philosophy be 'Christian'? What relationship is there between the constitutive 'Christian' revelation (in the Old and New Testaments and in the reinterpretation of tradition by the Christian community) as such and the social *institutions* which Christians have built up in the course of history, such as the family, the state, schools, etc.? See my *Ethics and Community*, Maryknoll, NY and Tunbridge Wells 1988, 21.

14. If one were to elaborate one basic criterion capable of maturing any given historical family institution 'from within', I should choose that of recognition of the other in 'face-to-face' (Hebrew *pnim-el-pnim*) encounter. Those who recognize in the Other another ethical subject who is the empirical presence of the Absolute, cannot turn him/her into a means. So men cannot turn women into mere economic means (as often happens in polygamy, for example), and, through living the Christian commandment of gratuitous love of the other (*agape*) from within existing structures, polygamy would gradually lose its 'cultural validity' – a traditional validity or acceptability that could not be challenged earlier for lack of a higher critical ethical principle or criterion. 'Evangelization' of existing family structures (from African polygamy to the egoist nuclear family of European late capitalism), in respect for and recognition of the other (of wife/mother: the widow; of daughter/son: the orphan; of grandmother/grandfather: the old as poor – as in the texts of *The Law of Hammurabi* or Isaiah), will be carried out through moving beyond existing relationships *to* a Christian praxis realized in community. No one historical structure (including the 'Christian' family put forward in Roman encyclicals) is an absolute ideal, nor can it replace Christian striving to move beyond all the limitations of a particular existing situation *from within*, working from a revealed critical ethic that *can never be fixed as an institution in history*, but that always has the capacity for moving beyond, for liberating.

15. Which means that separation is possible for reasons other than those given to justify it in the *Catholic Code of Canon Law* (which is clearly not 'revealed'). For example, the article 'Marriage' in *DTC* IX, 1926, 2044–335, traces a history of the institution (without reference to Africa, Asia or Latin America), in which it states that the *Code of Hummurab*, law 145, stipulated that a husband could take a concubine if his wife had not given him a son, although in this case the concubine would not have the rank of a wife. This tradition was fulfilled by Abraham (Gen. 30.3). Polygamy is an accepted institution in the Old Testament (Deut. 21.15–17; Judg. 8.30; II Kings 2.2); Solomon had hundreds of wives, with still no pronouncement against polygamy. With Paul, especially the famous text about women obeying their husbands (Eph. 5.22–23, which *still* fails to criticize the male-dominated institution of Greco-Roman culture), one should take care not to confuse such statements with 'revealed' truths: that is, this statement is not a revealed criterion or principle of Christian ethics; to call it such would be a most unfortunate confusion. This is why Jesus permits a woman to be put away for adultery or bad conduct (Matt. 5.31–32; 19.1–9), and the same was allowed in the early church (*DTC*, here 2059), though remarriage was not. Paul indicates that a woman cannot put away her husband, which is unbalanced. Paul also gives his personal opinion that a marriage contracted before becoming a Christian is not indissoluble (I Cor. 7.12–15). The church gradually institutionalized the marriage of Mediterranean culture. The Council of Arles in 341 repeated that men who put their wives aside for adultery cannot remarry; a consecrated virgin cannot validly marry; marriage between a Christian and a pagan is not allowed, etc. The Nestorian council of Mar Aba in 544 condemned bigamy and polyandry (though still not polygamy), set limits of consanguinity, etc. (*DTC*, 2116). It can be said that Latin European marriage began in the eleventh century in the West (though not in the whole of Christendom: *DTC*, 2135ff.). The process culminated with the restoration of Roman law under the seal of Christendom in the Gregorian reform. But this form *should never be confused with 'Christian' marriage*, which is continually being made 'from within' existing structures.

16. *DTC*, 2062.

17. 'When polygamy was a common custom, it was no crime (*contra mores*); it ranks as a crime now because it is no longer customary. We must distinguish between offences against nature, offences against common custom, offences against positive law' (*Contra Faustum Manich.*, xxii, 47). If there are indigenous Latin American, Asian and African family customs accepted since antiquity and still in existence, Augustine and Thomas Aquinas (for whom polygamy was justified when its purpose was procreation) would agree that the above quotation is rigorist, and false in its supposedly universal actual application.

18. See Pablo Richard, *Death of Christendoms, Birth of the Church*, Maryknoll, NY 1987; also my 'The Expansion of Christendom, its Crisis and the Present Moment', *Concilium* 144, 1981, 44–50.

19. See the treatment of the subject in my *Toward the Myth of Modernity. The Eclipse of the Other*, New York 1995.

20. See E. Dussel (ed.), *The Church in Latin America 1492–1992*, Tunbridge Wells and Maryknoll, NY, esp. 43–52.

21. See my article 'Modern Christianity in the Face of the "Other": from the "Rude" Indian to the "Noble Savage"', *Concilium* 130, 1979, 49–59.

22. For example, among the Incas the triple commandment *Ama Llulla, Ama Kella, Ama Sua* ('Thou shalt not lie, Thou shalt not be idle, Thou shalt not steal') ruled the

whole of life and was strictly and universally observed. The 'Thou shalt not lie', meaning not be hypocritical, included married fidelity, condemnation of adultery, etc. The Inca-Quechua people were never again to have such a rigorous or well-observed ethic as they had *before the conquest and so-called evangelization*. The process of colonization was ethically destructive.

23. Octavio Paz narrates the tragedy of the 'son of nobody', left alone (rejected by his violent Spanish father Hernán Cortés and refusing his mother, Malinche, the Indian woman who was given to the *conquistador*, for betraying her country), in *Laberintos de la Soledad*, Mexico City 1950. See my *Liberación de la mujer y erótica latinoamericana*, Bogotá 1990. On the religious life of the family in the colonial period in Latin America see my 'La vida cotidiana de la cristiandad', in *Historia General de la Iglesia en América Latina*, I/1, Salamanca 1983, 561–607; on Brazil, see Eduardo Hoornaert, 'A Familia', in *Historia da Igreja no Brasil* I/1, Petrópolis 1977, 370ff.; also Hans-J. Prien, 'Colonización y misión', in *La Historia del Cristianismo en América Latina*, Salamanca 1985, 75–88.

24. See *Pro Mundi Vita* 38, 1971, 25.

25. The first president of Argentina, Justo J. Urquiza, boasted in 1850 that he had more than fifty children by various women – and much the same went for all political leaders of the period.

26. See. e.g., *Sex, Love and Marriage in the Caribbean*, Geneva 1964: in Jamaica 76% of children are 'illegitimate' (p. 15); also Raymond Smith, *The Negro Family in British Guiana*, New York and London 1956; Judith Blake, *Family Structure in Jamaica*, New York 1961.

27. See, *inter alia*, Jorge Maldonado, 'Evangelicalism and the Family in Latin America', *International Review of Mission* 82, 1993, 189–202; John Burdick, 'Gossip and Secrecy: Women's Articulation of Domestic Conflict', *Sociological Analysis* 51, 1990, 153–70; Luis Lenero, 'Crísis del modelo nuclear-conyugal en los países latinoamericanos'. *Pro Mundi Vita* 21, 1980, 1–48; 'La familia y pastoral en América Latina', *Pro Mundi Vita Dossier 1*, 1976, 65–94.

28. This subject is dealt with in another article in this issue, so I have kept my observations short. But see Mercy A. Oduyoye in *One in Christ* 25, 1989, 238–54; John Pobee (ed.), *Religion, Morality and Population Dynamics*, Ghana 1974; Luc Hertsens, 'Family and Marriage among Christians in Sub-Saharan Africa', *Pro Mundi Vita, Africa Dossier 2*, 1970, 1–62. The 1980 Synod was important: see Brian Hearne, 'Synod of Bishops 1980', *AFER* 23, 1981, 1–128; Kweshi Bimwenyi, 'L'Afrique au Synode: problème de la famille', *Bulletin de Théologie Africaine* 4, 1982, 55–73; Benezeri Kisembo, *African Christian Marriage*, London 1977; also Arthur Phillips (ed.), *Survey of African Marriage and Family Life*, Dublin 1964; *All-Africa Seminar on the Christian Home and Family Life*, London 1953; John Robinson, *The Family Apostolate and Africa*, Geneva 1963; Cuthbert Omari, 'The Emerging Family Structures in Tanzania and the Work of the Church', *Africa Theological Journal* 19, 1990, 21–37.

29. See David and Vera Mace, *Marriage: East and West*, New York 1960; Jacob S. Quiambao, *The Asian Family in a Changing Society*, Quezon City 1965; Rjah Manikam (ed.), *The Christian Family in Changing East Asia*, Manila 1955; etc.

30. See Jacqueline Trincaz, 'Christianisme, Islam et transformations sociales', *Archives de Sciences Sociales de Religions* 23, 1978, 85–109; M. Haddad, 'The Double Role of Churches among Christian Arabs in Jordan', *Muslim World* 82, 1992, 67, 89.

Dorothy Blitsten, *The World of the Family*, New York 1963, bibliography 281–91, deals with the subject of the Muslim family (190–229); cf. Irfan Orga, *Portrait of a Turkish Family*, New York 1950. Muslim families, descendants of the desert nomads, have a strong clan 'belonging', formerly needed for economic survival. Deeply rooted in the Qur'an and Islamic law, which has historically regulated actual family structure (which is not the case with the New Testament), they are structured as 'corporate families', true clans or tribes, cemented by 'contracts' or 'alliances' (agreed by the elders). When one part of these is broken, grave conflicts can arise. Families are patriarchal, with children absolutely subject; there is strict division of work, of space in the house, of privileges, etc. Celibacy is condemned and polygamy encouraged (up to four wives). Families are compassionate to widows and orphans and welcoming to strangers. In Turkey and Egypt polygamy and concubinage have been outlawed. In general, women suffer heavy oppression, serve their husbands sexually and do the housework.

31. See, e.g. Maung Maung, *Law and Custom in Burma and the Burmese Family*, The Hague 1963; *Sex, Marriage and the Family in the Pacific*, Geneva 1969; Emma Porio, *The Filipino Family*, Manila 1978; etc.

32. See George Kurian, *The Indian Family in Transition*, The Hague 1961; K. M. Kapadia, *Marriage and the Family in India*, Bombay 1958; Marie Mascarenhas, 'Die Christen und das Familienleben in modernen Indien', in E. Schambeck (ed.), *Apostolat und Familie*, Berlin 1980, 529–37; Manisha Roy, 'The Oedipus Complex and the Bengali Family in India', in T. Williams (ed.), *Psychological Anthropology*, The Hague 1975, 123–34; George Kurian, 'The Family in India', *Studies in the Social Sciences* 12, 1974: the whole issue is devoted to the subject.

33. R. P. Müller, 'La famille indienne dans les bouleversements spirituels et sociaux d'aujourdhui', in *Familles anciennes, familles nouvelles*, 193.

34. See Jan Bosco, 'Tradition et christianisme dans la vie familiale au Punjab', in ibid., 173ff.

35. See D. Blitsten, 'Corporate Family in Confucian China', in *The World of the Family*, 82–113: '[the clan is] made up of a series of partially autonomous extended families guided by executive and administrative councils of elders' (83), comprising thousands of members, who can be dispersed in relatively distant parts. The basic functional unity extends over three generations, but the clan extends to five generations and even to collateral ramifications with a sixth. It should not be forgotten that the family cult of 'ancestors' is the central rite in the whole of Chinese culture. In practice the old traditions are observed completely only by the upper classes. The poor cannot maintain such extended relationships (through lack of money, mobility, etc.).

36. See Aline Kan, 'Marriage and the Family in China, 1949–1969'. *IDOC -Internazionale* 34, 1971, 71–96.

37. The missionary vision of the great Jesuit missionary Matteo Ricci, who began his work in China in 1601, was to see that the family was central to Chinese religion, and he rightly judged that ancestor worship was not contrary to the gospel. But Rome condemned this creative missionary project out of deep 'Eurocentrism'. I have examined this question in 'La querella de los ritos', *HGIAL*, I/1, 350ff.

38. Such as, for example, the situation of the family in the ex-USSR, now Russia (see, e.g., Rudolph Schlesinger, *The Family in the USSR*, London 1949), because for a few short years the institution of the family was supposedly abolished (but had to be reconstituted in 1930 because of the resulting chaos); or in Israel (see e.g. Melfor E.

Spiro, *Venture in Utopia*, Cambridge, Mass. 1956; id., *Children of the Kibbutz*, Cambridge, Mass. 1958) where varied experiments in family organization were carried out in the Kibbutzim, from fully communal living (which was soon abandoned), to Jewish religious and believing communities, in which life seemed to be carried on as in veritable monasteries of farming families.

39. 'Valid' comes from 'validity', which means what is generally accepted by common consent, sanctioned by custom and, though it can be falsified, is held by all to be 'true'. The intersubjective and cultural 'validity' of an institution is the starting point for an 'evangelization' of the family, rather than a mere *outside* critique from an ideal impossible in other cultures (an ideal that is no more than the European family projected as the 'Christian' family).

40. There are examples of this stance: 'One of the Moravian missionaries defended the polyandry of the Tibetans, not as an institution worthy of being approved of *in theory or tolerated among Christians*[!], but as being good for pagans living in such a barren country', 'Familie', *LGE* 16, 1148. What happens is that every 'theory' changes over time through the maturing of the ethical-cultural understanding of Christians who themselves formulated the theory, but find that when they actually 'encounter' a strange people, they cannot *ipso facto* demand that they accept another stage of development which is incomprehensible within the terms of their culture.

The Family and Moral Decisions: How should the Christian Family Respond to the New Moral Challenges of Today?

Marifé Ramos González

Introduction

Before attempting to answer this question, we must make two important points:

(a) There is no such thing as *'the* Christian family'. There are millions of Christian families whose moral decisions are affected by the social, economic, political and religious conditions of the culture in which they live. These conditions help or hinder such families to take decisions which are more or less creative. They determine their attitude to Christian moral teaching and strengthen or weaken their bond with the church. 'The Christian family' has been over-simplified and excessively idealized. Unfortunately, each family's particular circumstances, which affect its moral decisions for better or worse, are often ignored.

(b) Many Christian families do not live their moral lives as a response to a personal calling but as behaviour imposed from outside. God observes this behaviour 'from outside and above'. Responding to moral challenges becomes as difficult as walking on shifting sands.

These families have not yet discovered the joy of experiencing moral life as a freely chosen path, in which God is a companion on their journey, who encourages, impels, welcomes and forgives them.

Are we Christian communities aware of the importance of living our moral lives as a joyful response? Do moral education teachers emphasize this aspect sufficiently?

Spanish Christian families are responding in many ways to the new moral challenges. This response requires more detailed study. Here I shall just point out three significant and widespread attitudes, which I introduce and explore in this article by means of a parable.

A community leader was depressed because he could not make his people's moral behaviour conform to what he had been preaching to them for many years. He had tried everything he could think of: long speeches, clear rules, severe prohibitions, threats . . . but all in vain.

Finally he decided to resort to the Ancient Bringer of Wisdom, who listened to him attentively, silently considered what he had said and then replied:

'How do you expect them to come, if they are so far off that they have not heard your religious call? Why do you dictate your rules to them, if they are offering you their music? Why don't you show them the goal, rather than erecting hurdles along the way?'

1. 'How do you expect them to come, if they are so far off that they have not heard your religious call?'

If we are convinced through personal experience of the richness of Christian moral teaching, we are bound to be pained by the situation of so many families who, although they have been baptized, still live immoral or amoral lives. These people are vaguely aware of the church's official moral teaching, through the media and the religious education they received in childhood. But this education is not put into practice and has no solid foundation. Worse still, they are ignorant of the gospel and are not conscious of having any very deep or intense religious experiences.

'How do you expect them to come?'

How can we demand that their lives should be a response if they do not hear God calling them by name, if their faith does not involve a relationship of trust? These are precisely the people who have the greatest difficulty in responding to moral challenges. Often they live for years with a dulled conscience, which only wakes up screaming at critical moments: when death is near, or in the face of suffering, or when life has no meaning.

How can we say to these families living immoral lives that Jesus is telling them: 'Neither do I condemn you . . . '? This saying does not lead to licence, as some excessively prudent people would have us believe. The saying jolts those who have encountered Christ, it upsets them, gets them going, burns into them . . . For those who have not encountered Christ, morality goes on being merely a set of rules.

Why do so many families not hear the call?

First and foremost because of the short-sighted anthropology underpinning many lectures on moral theology, a view of human nature and what is natural, which many Christian families find difficult or impossible to accept. Neither men nor women recognize themselves in the models proposed.

The second reason is that the language in which moral rules and values are described is seriously obscure. The search for more precise technical terms has sacrificed clarity, to the point where many moral texts have become incomprehensible jargon for the people of God.

The third reason is that the places where morality is 'worked out' are distant and detached (in every sense) from the daily lives of millions of Christian families. Paul VI called the lay men and women attending the Council 'experts in life'. Therefore it is important to include lay men and women in the task of enriching moral theology through the experience of daily life, through reflection on its rich significance and the joys and sorows of couples of families.

Because they do not hear this call, many Christian families have given up the practice of their religion. Their membership of the church gradually declines and they feel 'condemned' when they look at their lives in the light of the church's moral teaching. This attitude is clearly and most dramatically seen in the case of persons, couples or families with addictions. Their response to moral challenges is to abandon the church, even though deep down they may still hold on to their religious beliefs. How can we build bridges for these people?

In the Middle Ages bridge-building was considered to be a work of mercy, because rivers, streams and ravines hinder people on their journey. Building bridges is still a work of mercy and a way of proving our Christian commitment today. It can help these Christian families to hear the call to a higher moral life. People in charge of Christian communities, leaders of family movements, we women and men theologians, all have the task of shortening distances, using other kinds of language, offering new anthropologies; the task of working to ensure that the call to live a moral life, as a response, can be heard and is not muted or obliterated by trivial summons to absurd and out-of-date behaviour.

In this attempt at a cordial approach we may face two temptations:

(a) We may want to shorten distances by clear and offensive rules, for example, to use excommunication. But rule-keeping out of fear does not help in the other great task of living a moral life as a joyful response.

(b) We may forget that we have to be prepared to 'meet people half way'. We cannot sit comfortably in our armchairs waiting for far-off men and women to struggle along the difficult path. The parable of the Prodigal Son is a reminder of what the Father does. He goes out of doors, and impatiently scans the horizon with open arms.

Let us hope we shall greet the millennium with a big welcome for Christian families, stressing our need to help them, in any way we can, to hear the call, instead of wasting our energies in broadcasting rules.

2. What is the music that many Christian families offer?

(a) They bear witness to the fact that the universe is like a great womb, of which we are part. They not only educate people in respect and care for nature, recycle enthusiastically and live frugally. They also remind us that 'we are nature and we are the universe'.

(b) They welcome multicultural and ethnic rich diversity. Their moral goal is to 'love what is different'. Their inner music leads them cordially to welcome the values which under-developed or developing countries offer decadent Europe.

(c) A new balance in male and female roles. This puts paid to injustices like women's double or triple working day and sole responsibility for child-care.

Women's gradual awakening in every cultural sphere is an outlet for their inner music, especially when this awakening does not lead them to seek revenge but progressively to dismantle the structure of the patriarchal family, which is so rigid in our countries. Women are exploring the implications of living in friendship, like brothers and sisters, like Jesus of Nazareth. And this 'community of equals' is put into practice in the family.

Changing roles and the new role-sharing are not a feminist demand but a moral decision affecting the structure of the family. It requires an awareness that the harmonious growth of every family member depends on it.

This growth is not without certain dangers:

– Economic growth should not be at the expense of family life, shared leisure and care for children, handicapped and old people.

– Intellectual growth of men should not be at the expense of women, who remain in their shadow and sacrifice their own development.

– Women's professional growth should not mean they cannot form a couple or have children, because these are perceived as obstacles to personal development.

Economic self-sufficiency has stifled many Western families, who have all the necessitites of life but lack the vital wealth of relaxed human relationships, shared festivals and an open home. East and South have a music which helps us to grow in harmony and community.

(d) A serene acceptance of the different response-rhythms in any given family (normally as many responses as there are family members). Encouragement of free personal responses, not those most pleasing to fathers and mothers.

(f) Having time for others and community life as indispensable moral values.

(g) Opposing the immorality of economic waste in those families who offer their sons and daughters an 'education' which simply encourages them to gain certificates and prestige, and to be competitive. Inner personal growth, self-discovery and social commitment through work are all neglected.

We are called to live moral lives inspired by our inner music, to open new paths, to improvise on the written score. Moral theologians, both male and female, have the specific task of helping couples and families discover this inner music.

3. Why don't you show them the goal, rather than erecting hurdles along the way?

We believe that hurdles are put up:

– When people like B. Häring are accused, because they have helped to show the merciful face of moral theology, which has been a blessing to so many families.

– When the church closes ranks round certain moral principles, and approaches fundamentalism.

– When it proposes a single model for the family and ignores the particularities of sex, race and culture. Although the church values the great diversity of gifts in the religious life (which leads some people to go and live in poor districts and others in the desert), it is nevertheless nervous of the cultural differences in families.

People are shown the goal (the Goal) when the Second Vatican Council reminds married people of the important task they have been called upon to perform: 'As they are called to give life, married couples share in the creative power of God's fatherhood (cf. Eph. 3.14; Matt. 23.9).' 'In their duty to pass on human life and educate their offspring, which they should consider as their special mission, husbands and wives known that they are co-operators in God the Creator's love, and in a way they are his interpreters. Hence, performing this task is a human and Christian responsibility'.[1]

Being co-operators and interpreters of God the Creator's love is a great calling. Upon the Christian couple's response depend not only their happiness but their salvation.

But a hurdle is erected along the way when it is presented as intrinsically evil to take 'any action which either in preparation for, or in the carrying out of, the conjugal act or in the development of its natural consequences, attempts, as an end or a means, to make procreation impossible'.[2]

'To the natural language expressing mutual total self-giving of the spouses, contraception imposes an objectively contradictory language, that is, not giving the whole self. The result is not only the positive rejection of openness to life, but also the falsification of the inner truth of conjugal love, which is called upon to give of itself in personal fullness.'[3]

When they keep bumping into hurdles placed along their way, many people end up turning to compulsions and addictions (food, drink, games, sex, etc.).

It would be better to show the goal by giving examples of couples and families who climb day by day up the path of holiness. Does the present disproportion in the Calendar of Saints between the numbers of virgins (priests, monks and nuns) and married people really reflect each group's striving for holiness, or isn't it rather an indication of the way in which beatification processes are pursued? If this is the case, the church is losing the witness and example of great lay men and women, whether married or not, who climbed to the top along new upward paths.

Few things have as great an effect as the example of those who follow Jesus through difficult moral decisions, made coherently and with love. As just one example, we may mention those couples who adopt children with Aids. They know that their lives will be full of sacrifices and setbacks as the disease takes its course. They know they may lose the child they love as a son or daughter. And despite this they still adopt them.

Another good example is given by those families who make space in their home, at their table and in their hearts, for people who are marginalized, for whatever reason. Or families who go to a third world country, risking their own health in order to bring health and life. Or persons who risk their lives, through hunger strikes or demonstrations (with all the consequences that can be imagined for their partner and children), in order to denounce the world's injustice and abuses of human rights.

The Catholic Church usually puts forward families with many children as exemplary. But these other families mentioned above show us the goal, because they have 'the mind of Christ': they share their bread with the hungry, shelter the homeless, break unjust chains . . . They make marriage credible, not as an archaic institution, but as a shared project, which empowers both husband and wife and is a source of joy. They show that there are other kinds of fruitfulness in family life. But these families are not paid due attention in the local, national or international community of the church.

Therefore it is very important that moral theology should become less abstract and progressively incorporate the witness of those who are climbing to the summit with enthusiasm, those families whose responses to the moral challenges of today are filled with coherence, creativity, risk and enthusiasm.

4. Conclusions

We return to the fundamental question we asked at the beginning: how are Christian families responding to the new moral challenges of today?

To the challenge of living frugally and sharing bread with the hungry the response is a minimalist morality, which falls far short of the real possibilities of a welfare society in the First World.

To the challenges of equality (between men and women, between citizens of different countries, ethnic groups etc), the response is a pharisaical morality. Here Jesus might well repeat his saying: 'Do what they say but not what they do . . .' (Matt. 23.3). Side by side with the proclamation of the great principles of equality, we find the incoherence of what goes on in daily life. Proof of this is given every day in the media, which report rapes and physical attacks on women, fathers and mothers who do not want gipsies to go to the same school as their children, violent outbreaks of racism, xenophobia etc. Working for equality within the family and between families remains a painful challenge to be faced.

It is difficult to find an adequate expression to reflect the response to the challenges of sexual morality. There is a lack of courage, and no structures exist for a fruitful dialogue between families and the hierarchy of the church which would enrich the theology of marriage and the family. The time has come to emerge from lethargy and passivity. It is time to accompany the young, couples and families to help them discover values, alleviate meaningless burdens and awaken a moral response.

'Lay Catholics have the right and sometimes even the duty, through their own special knowledge, competence and prestige, to tell the clergy their opinions about what pertains to the good of the church and to make them clear to other Catholics, saving always the integrity of faith and custom, and respect for the clergy, and taking into account what is useful to the community and the dignity of persons.'[4]

The concept of 'family' is becoming suffocatingly restricted in some industrialized countries. It has been reduced to the nucleus of parents and children. Sometimes the family consists only of father or mother and one son or daughter. We have a lot to learn from cultures in which the concept of the family is much broader and includes relations and neighbours, and takes particular care of weaker members. Because we are all children of the same God (Father and Mother), we are driven constantly to break out of our narrow concept of the family towards the great universal family.

There is also an inadequate response to the challenge of praying about all moral decisions, including them in our personal and family conversation with God. There should and could be a more fruitful relationship between family spirituality and moral life, because they are root and trunk of the same tree: the following of Jesus of Nazareth.

Let us hope that we Christian families gradually respond creatively to the new challenges, and can relate our faithfulness to Jesus' message to new ways of living as a family. Let us hope we become aware of the great challenge: to live a moral life which is a joyful response to a personal call by Someone who 'stands before and behind us and has his hand on us' (Ps. 139).

Translated by Dinah Livingstone

Notes

1. *Gaudium et spes* 50.2; *Catechism of the Catholic Church*, no. 2367.
2. *Humanae vitae* 14.
3. FC 32.
4. *Catechism of the Catholic Church*, no. 907.

The Family in the Teaching of the Magisterium

Norbert Mette

I. The focus on the family

'Pope warns against threat of dissolution of the family', 'The church must defend the traditional family' – these and similar lurid headlines about church statements on the family, which can be read time and again in the press, have multiplied notably in the past 'Year of the Family'. They are an indication of the degree to which the family is at the centre of the magisterium's attention and pastoral concern. At the same time they convey something of the tone which can often be heard in expressions of the church's concern for the family: anxiety about growing hostility to the family which is regarded as a product of modern society and the process of secularization, and which is expected to lead not only to the gradual collapse of the family but ultimately to the downfall of human civilization.[1] This particular 'concern' is also a result of the introduction of the feast of the Holy Family into the liturgical calendar in 1921.[2] The pastoral letters written for 'Family Sundays' since then have continually confirmed this with striking condemnations of the spirit of the time, presented as being destructive of the family, and passionate appeals for the preservation of the family combined with fierce threats of sanctions.[3]

In pastoral practice, during the course of this century orientation on the family has increasingly displaced the differentiation by 'natural states' (wives, husbands, children) which had been customary earlier and in part has been deliberately encouraged at quite considerable expense. The significance attached to this concern of the whole church also emerges from the fact that the 'Committee for the Family' which was established in 1973 by Pope Paul VI was elevated in 1980 by the present pope to become the

'Papal Council for the Family', with the task of seeing to the dissemination of the church's teaching on the family, encouraging and co-ordinating pastoral efforts in this sphere, and stimulating the development of studies on family spirituality. This council is especially to be concerned with efforts to pursue a practice of responsible parenthood in the church and to provide help in this direction. Special theological Family Institutes have been established (in Rome and Roermond) to intensify research in this area.

What (theological) view of the family governs this pastoral concern for the family? In this article I shall summarize it and subject it to a critical evalution.

II. Catholic teaching on the family

Since the most concise form of the binding teaching of the Catholic Church is at present to be found in the *Catechism of the Catholic Church*, I shall summarize briefly the essential definitions which are given there:[4]

(*a*) A family is made up of 'a man and a woman united in marriage' (2202) and their children. Its foundation and thus its basic constitution derive from God's creation. In this respect it 'is prior to any recognition by public authority, which has an obligation to recognize it' (ibid.)

(*b*) The family forms the 'original cell' of social life: 'It is the natural society in which husband and wife are called to give themselves in love and in the gift of life. Authority, stability and a life of relationships within the family constitute the foundations for freedom, security and fraternity within society. The family is the community in which, from childhood, one can learn moral values, begin to honour God and make good use of freedom. Family life is an initiation into life in society' (2207). Because of its fundamental significance, the family 'must be helped and defended by appropriate social measures' (2209).

(*c*) Christian faith emphasizes the significance of the family by seeing in it 'a sign and image of the communion of the Father and the Son in the Holy Spirit' (2205) which reflects the creative work of God in the procreation and education of children. As a 'community of faith, hope and love' (2204), the Christian family is 'a specific revelation and realization of ecclesial communion' (2204), and for this reason 'it can and should be called a domestic church' (1655ff., 2204). Thus the family is 'the first school of Christian life' (1657).

(*d*) 'For the common good of its members and of society, the family necessarily has manifold responsibilities, rights and duties' (2203). More specifically this on the one hand includes the 'duties of children' (2241ff.)

to respect their parents, to show gratitude to them, to obey them and to look after them materially and morally in old age, sickness and need. Conversely, the 'duties of parents' (2221) consist in bringing up their children, making a home for them, giving them an example of a holy life and also explicitly introducing them to the faith. Parents have a right to the free choice of a school for their children.

(e) Those who are prevented from marrying and having a family or who deliberately choose not to in order to contribute 'to the good of the human family' (2231) in another way may not be discriminated against (cf. also 1658). In particular – it is again said explicitly under the heading 'The Family and the Kingdom' (sic, 2232f.) – 'family ties are not absolute' where there is a 'special vocation which comes from God' (2232); in this case the kingdom of God stands before and over the family. (This point will not be commented on further; note, however, the understanding of the kingdom of God expressed in this section of the *Catechism*.)

As a basis for this doctrine of the family, reference is made in the notes on the text to relevant biblical passages and to resolutions of the Second Vatican Council (*Lumen gentium, Gaudium et spes, Gravissimum educationis*) and above all to the Apostolic Brief of John Paul II, *Familiaris Consortio*, on the tasks of the Christian family in today's world (1981). The 'Letter to Families' (1994) composed by the present pope on the occasion of the Year of the Family can also be added as an official declaration.

If this somewhat spiritual letter is directed primarily to Catholic families, another Vatican document of recent times makes it clear that the terms of the Catholic teaching on the family are by no means limited to members of this church but that its content is normative for the family generally. This is the 'Charter of Family Rights' which the Holy See presented in 1983 to 'all persons, institutions and authorities which are concerned with the mission of the family in today's world'. In the introduction to this charter, which also represents a compendium of the church's social teaching on the topics concerned, summed up in twelve articles, we read: 'The rights proclaimed in this charter are contained in the human conscience and in the shared values of all humankind. Here the Christian aspect is given by the light of the divine revelation which illuminates the reality of the family given by nature. In the last resort these rights grow out of that law which the creator has inscribed on the hearts of all men and women. Society is called on to defend these rights against all violations and to heed and encourage them to the full.'

III. The scope and limits of the magisterium's doctrine of the family

As described above, in the texts of the magisterium the family – like marriage, and to some degree as its 'consequence' – is attributed to the creative will of God and thus is defined as being fundamentally rooted in the order of creation. It is thus an original and distinctive social form which is not derived from other institutions – either by society or by the church. Quite clearly it has an influence beyond itself and makes an essential contribution to the shaping of human social life in other spheres. It need not be disputed that this theological model of the family, which is strongly stamped by natural law and is based on a deductive argument, contains some important insights. That is especially evident where the question is asked how the ideal of the family can be fulfilled in reality and where there is reflection on the presuppositions which must be fulfilled for this to be done as well as possible. In this way, priority is given to the material and social-political conditions which are necessary if family life is to be made possible: for example the demand for a 'family wage' which has been made in social encyclicals since *Rerum novarum*; the demand for appropriate living conditions; the demand for a policy which is particularly concerned for the interests of the family.[5] In some of these areas pressure from the church has been in the forefront of influencing the formation of the political will and contributing to an improvement in the situations of families.

However, the model sketched out above proves quite inadequate when it is not just a question of presuppositions like this but of a view and understanding of the full reality of the family.[6] The reason for that is that the model:

– Asserts that the family is a structure beyond time and context, whereas it is no such thing. A mere look at the biblical writings is enough to show the very different forms the family has taken at different times and in different cultures. Fundamentally, the model based on natural law asserts nothing less than a specific form of the family, of the kind that has developed in the course of modernity, above all in Europe and North America, the so-called middle-class family, the characteristics of which are:[7] the family as a natural organism, the original cell of state and society, on the frontier between the public and private spheres, with a clear structure of authority.

– Sees the family as a completely static entity and is quite simply blind to the inner dynamic which is characteristic of family life and which follows simply from the fact that the courses of development of those involved are as a rule anything but uniform.

– Regards the family as a pre-existing ordinance the normative expression of which can be found, say, in the commandments of God (above all the Fourth Commandment) and consequently leaves only very limited room for its shaping. And finally,

– Thinks of the family almost exclusively in terms of the institution of marriage between husband and wife which is the foundation for it. But even leaving aside the fact that as a result the kind of detachment of marriage from family which has taken place (and not just today) in the course of the pluralization of forms of the family is *a priori* labelled illegitimate, this is no way of understanding the family as a distinctive social and psychological reality differing from marriage in structure and function. In theological terms, the family often remains a secondary entity: after all, it is marriage which is given the sacramental dignity and which therefore as a rule is reflected on with greater intensity. Here, too, there is a tendency to derive the family as a theological reality from marriage.

The Second Vatican Council attempted to correct this doctrine of the family based on natural law by prompting further development above all in two directions. First, with its recognition of the understanding of marriage and family that has emerged in recent times and is often already being practised, in which the traditional patriarchal image has been replaced with a form of life stamped by partnership (cf. above all *Gaudium et Spes* 48). This aspect has been echoed widely in the pastoral and theological reception of the council and, as can be shown from various documents produced by local churches,[8] has been developed very consistently. Instead of a focus on the institutional character of the family, attention is now increasingly being paid to its complex structure of relationships. The sometimes very rigid normative definitions are being replaced by an approach orientated more on everyday life together.[9] Secondly, there is a revaluation of the ecclesiological significance of the family when it is said to be the 'domestic sanctuary of the church' (*Apostolicum actuositatem*, 11), 'a kind of domestic church' (*Lumen gentium* 11).

Even if the same terms are used, and sometimes the council texts are quoted literally, it is unmistakable that the doctrine of the family in the *Catechism* falls far behind the genuine intentions of the council: here the institutional and normative perspective has again come to set the tone. There is something to be said for attributing this lapse to that paradoxical-seeming process in which the theology of the family presented in embryo by the Second Vatican Council has been taken up and developed by the supreme authority of the church. As one might pointedly remark, this is sometimes 'too little', and sometimes 'too much'.

By 'too little' I mean that above all with the encyclical *Humanae vitae* (1968) and its aftermath the topic of the family was more or less limited to the question of 'family planning'. At the same time the argument from natural law reached a new peak. By 'too much' I mean that not least in order to make up for the anthropological and theological deficiencies of the 'family planning morality' imposed by the magisterium, Pope John Paul II initially in *Familiaris consortio* and explicitly in his 1994 'Letter to Families' has portrayed an ideal of the family on the basis of his personalistic thought, steeped in the theology of revelation, which in ever new approaches and with ever more lofty formulations evokes and transfigures the family as a community of persons grounded in and ensouled by love, the origin and goal of which is the 'divine We'.

The pernicious character of such thought and language does not stem only from the fact that such an abstract truth can hardly be communicated by family life – unless it could permanently take the harmonious and pious form which the pope probably imagines it to have; the imprisonment in romanticizing exaggerations and the inability to perceive relationships as they really exist also all too obviously favours an attitude which interprets any deviation from the ideal as a collapse and condemns it morally. The various situations of partners and families which are stigmatized as 'irregular' (cf. *Familiaris consortio*, 79–84) cannot then be looked at and assessed in a differentiated way, but are all regarded as the symptom of a social development which is branded decadent and pathological. They thus fall victim to the sweeping verdict that is passed on the forces which cause and further this development. Internally it is also the case that the concerns for a differentiated understanding of the reality of marriage and the family, which has now become pluralistic, and for a pastoral solution which takes account of this, have come under suspicion of giving way to relativistic tendencies and dissolving the truth.[10] The 'Christian family' as the *Catechism* prescribes it, as being binding on the whole of Catholic Christianity,[11] must stand as a bulwark against the forces of disintegration in the present.

There should be no disputing the fact that a series of tendencies listed by the pope – the spread of the consumerist hedonistic attitude to life combined with materialist utilitarian thinking; a decline in the capacity for community and the readiness for solidarity; a degradation of sexuality (and in this connection above all of women, as objects of pleasure, etc.) – are in fact to the point. But it is too much also to want to derive a collapse of the family directly from this. If we follow the findings of sociologists, what can be noted, rather, is a remarkable stability in the family today; and even the rise of new and alternative forms of family is by no means as large as widespread opinion would suggest.[12] What most certainly has happened is a far-reaching change in the structure and function of the family. While this is still not perceived – and Vatican II at least began to become aware of the fact – and instead the perspective remains rooted in a traditionalist image of the family, it is not surprising that the statements of the magisterium are seen by the persons concerned as being blind to reality, and dismissed as being not much help.

IV. Towards the revision of central themes of the magisterium – two examples

I shall attempt to demonstrate the possible consequences which could arise for church preaching and pastoral work on the family from two definitions which play a central role in the traditional doctrine.

1. The family as 'original cell'

The definition of the family as the '(original) cell' of society has become a classic theme of Catholic social teaching. Even if it is emphasized that this does not mean the view that all social structures are present in embryo in the family and take their departure from there, but that 'cell' must be understood in terms of the fundamental significance of the family for society both biologically and morally,[13] at the latest after the breakthrough of developed modernity such a definition proves problematical. As a consequence of the process of social differentiation, not only has every possible social part-system become independent so that the parts are capable of linking together only to a limited degree, but in addition the family-part system has come to be characterized quite decisively by a quality of social relationships which stands in abrupt opposition to the purely functional relationships which dominate elsewhere in inter-personal dealings. It is precisely this which results in the precarious situation of families in the present, so that more often than not they issue in failure.[14]

Possibly in this context there is still some justification of talking of the family as an 'original cell'. However, here we must be aware that in that case the intention runs counter to the facts. It does not represent conservative ideas of order but rather (prophetic) criticism of a society which tends to make the family the rubbish dump or workshop which repairs human damage done elsewhere, and leaves those concerned to their own resources in coping with it. The propagation of ideals is no help at all in such a situation. Rather, families need to be understood, and if possible given some solid support for the different balancing acts that they have to perform because of the different expectations pinned on them from outside and from within. In addition, there is need for a political lobby which intervenes effectively so that families can live up to the characteristic which is rightly attributed to them: 'a school for human enrichment' (*Gaudium et spes*, 52).

2. *The family as 'domestic church'*

A phrase which Vatican II took up somewhat hesitantly – following John Chrysostom in describing the family as a 'domestic church'[15] – has become established terminology in the post-Vatican documents that I have quoted, especially where the status of the family in the church is addressed. However, it should be noted that the original intention of the council, namely to revalue the ecclesiological significance of the family, has undergone a remarkable shift in accent. Instead of the family being evaluated in its original independence, the term 'domestic church' is used in an attempt to requisition the family for the institution in a lofty way. The 'spiritual packaging' conceals nothing less than the expectation that the 'Catholic family' is a reliable place for the reproduction of the church, and moreover functions as an advance bulwark of the 'fortress of God' against tendencies towards liberalization and pluralization.

The opportunities which could arise from an evaluation of the family as a 'domestic church' are thus lost. To understand them in fact presupposes[16] first recognizing and taking seriously the fact that with few exceptions the coalition between family and church still practised in past generations has been shattered (not least by what F.-X. Kaufmann has called the 'ecclesiasticization of Christianity'), and secondly a sensitivity to the fact that this dissociation of the family from the church by no means entails its total secularization. On the contrary, we can note that the family in particular has become a place which to an amazing degree is productive in religious matters – to the point of bearing an excessive religious load.[17]

In these changed circumstances, a new arrangement between church and family will come about only if the church (here understood as the 'official church') once and for all stops attempting to commandeer and supervise families and respects the autonomy that they have to fight for and preserve – laboriously enough – in order to be able to cope successfully with the very varied expectations pinned on them 'from outside' which can easily overtax them. If in this connection families direct their efforts towards finding a meaning which strengthens them in their precarious reality and take on various promising tasks in this direction, it is no help if all this is immediately disallowed and rejected as syncretism. Difficult though an individualized religion which comes about in this way may seem to an institutionalized church, it nevertheless contains some significant elements of a transformed Christianity. The church should be and must be concerned to detect this and to show solidarity with families in such quests – even, indeed precisely, if some fail in the process. In this way families will no longer be degraded into becoming copies of the existing institutional church. Rather, as a genuine field of experience for religion and faith they are places where time and again the church can and does come into being. When that happens, and for that reason, they deserve the designation 'domestic church'.[18]

V. Beginning from those concerned

The reflections above are an attempt not to let the deep gulf which has come into being between the magisterium's doctrine of the family and the reality of the family be the last word. Without wanting simply to argue for a normativity of the facts, I believe that it is high time that for both sides – for the Catholic church and for the family – this gulf should be bridged. For the church, if the maxim that the human being is the way of the church is not to remain just a gesture; for the family, if it is not to end up without any of the orientation or support which is helpful and sometimes necessary.

However, for this to happen it is necessary first of all for the existing doctrine to be 'earthed' again in reality as it is lived. Ecclesiastical and theological statements and actions will gain credibility in present-day conditions to the degree that they are not made 'from above', above the heads and hearts of those concerned, but together with them. The institutional church still comes into contact with families at many points and here in part it can sense quite directly something of their reality – in connection with the informal occasions connected with certain family events, through its offering of family education and catechesis and not least through its diaconal institutions (family counselling, material aid, etc). Here it has long been known that ideals are no help for normal family life with its ups and downs, its splits and reunions. It must be possible for faith, if it is not to remain a basically superfluous superstructure, to be spelt out in this everyday life, down to the basic needs of family solidarity which make themselves felt at different times. The fact that Christian faith is linked at a basic level to the longing of many people for experiences of trust, love and hope which they seek to have fulfilled in the family brings it very near to this form of life (without absolutizing a particular kind of it); it promises support for this longing which also gets lost in failure.[19] Who is called to bear authentic witness to such experiences more than those concerned?

Translated by John Bowden

Notes

1. A people 'in which marriage and family collapse is sooner or later doomed to destruction' (Pius XII, 24 July 1949), here quoted from U. Schmälzle, 'Kirche und Familie: Zur Wahrhnehmung gelebter Wirklichkeit', *Erwachsenenbildung* 40, 1994, 12–16: 12.
2. Cf. J. Lange, *Ehe- und Familienpastoral heute*, Vienna 1977, 211.
3. See the analysis of 253 German pastoral letters between 1915 and 1975 in U. Schmälzle, *Ehe und Familie im Blickpunkt der Kirche*, Freiburg im Breisgau 1979.
4. For what folllows see *The Catechism of the Catholic Church*, London 1994, esp.1655–58 and 2201–33.
5. Cf. the 'Charter of Family Rights' (it contains references to the texts of the various social encyclicals).
6. Cf. V. Eid, 'Elemente einer theologisch-ethischen Lehre über die Familie', in id. and L. Vascovics (ed.), *Wandel der Familie – Zukunft der Familie*, Mainz 1982, 179–200.
7. Cf. K. Lüscher and F. Böckle, 'Familie', *ChrGimG* 7, Freiburg im Breisgau 1981, 87–145: 95f.
8. For Germany cf. e.g. the resolution of the General Synod of Dioceses in the Federal Republic of Germany, 'Christlich gelebte Ehe und Familie' (*GSyn* I, 423–57), and the resolutions on the same topic passed by the diocesan synods of Hildesheim and Rottenburg-Stuttgart.
9. Cf. D. Mieth, 'Familienethos: Leitbilder und Problemlösungen für eine ethisch orientierte Erwachsenenbildung', in Eid and Vascovics (ed.), *Wandel der Familie – Zukunft der Familie* (n.6), 201–26; cf.also U. Baumann, *Utopie Partnerschaft*, Düsseldorf 1994.
10. Cf. e.g. recently (1994) the document from the Congregation for the Doctrine of Faith on the receiving of communion by divorced faithful who have remarried, which is a reaction to the principles put forward by the bishops of the church province of Upper Rhineland on the pastoral care of people with broken marriages, the divorced, and divorced persons who have remarried (Freiburg im Breisgau etc. 1993).
11. Cf. here the scanty remarks on 'inculturation' in *Familiaris consortio*, 10.
12. Cf. R. Nave-Herz, *Familie heute*, Darmstadt 1994.
13. Cf. J. Höffner, *Christliche Gesellschaftslehre*, Kevelaer 1963, 101ff.

14. Cf. K. Lüscher et al (eds.), *Die 'postmoderne' Familie*, Constance 1988.
15. Cf. E: Lodi, 'Famigilia – chiesa domestica nella tradizione patristica', *RivpatLit* 18, 1980, 221ff.
16. Cf. N. Mette, 'Die Familie als Kirche im kleinen', in Eid and Vascovics (ed.), *Wandel der Familie – Zukunft der Familie* (n.6), 263–83.
17. Cf. C. and K. Gabriel, 'Familie im gesellschaftlichen Überdruck', *Erwachsenenbildung* 49, 1994, 9ff.
18. Cf. also J.A.K. McGinnis, 'Family as Domestic Church', in J. Coleman (ed.), *One Hundred Years of Catholic Social Thought*, New York 1991, 120–34.
19. Cf. K. Neumann, 'An die Familie glauben?', *EE* 44, 1992, 242–7.

The Christian Family as Domestic Church at Vatican II

Michael A. Fahey

Almost imperceptibly in the Roman Catholic Church since the 1960s, the expression 'domestic church' has become a familiar way of describing the Christian family, especially the 'traditional' family encompassing husband and wife together with children. How and why this expression was introduced into modern church usage are questions few can answer. One Italian bishop, still living, according to the most recent *Annuario pontificio*, should be specifically credited for introducing the concept into the texts of Vatican II, although ironically he would have preferred the patristic expressions 'small church' or 'miniature church'. Since the publication of the complete *Acta* of Vatican II, we are now able to study the various drafts of the conciliar documents and to read in full the episcopal interventions such as those of Fiordelli that led to revisions.

When Vatican II opened on 11 October 1962, considerable work on a draft document on the church had already been completed. Its authors, members of the Doctrinal Commission, expected a speedy ratification of the text without much ado.[1] During the first session of the council, however, it became clear that this initial draft did not meet the expectations of the majority of the council fathers. The *Schema de Ecclesia* was printed and distributed at the Council only on 23 November 1962, during the twenty-fifth working session, technically known as a General Congregation. Cardinal Ottaviani, on 1 December, introduced the draft containing 11 chapters, 45 points and some 123 folio pages. After only a few days of discussion, the council fathers voted for a complete overhaul of the text, and to assist in that process expanded the Doctrinal Commission. Persons who wished to submit suggested drafts to the Commission were encouraged to do so in writing during the months between the end of the first session (December 1962) and the opening of the second session (September 1963).

The major inspiration at Vatican II behind the special focus on the family as a 'minuscule church' or 'domestic church' was Bishop Pietro Fiordelli of Prato, Italy, whose priestly ministry had included considerable involvement in the Christian Family Movement.[2] His contributions to the council's Dogmatic Constitution on the Church, including several ideas that were not adopted in the final text, came in three stages: a brief and interrupted oral intervention on 5 December 1962; a written submission between the first and the second session; and a speech on 17 October 1963, during a lively conciliar debate. All these texts are easily accessible in Latin in the published *Acta synodalia* of Vatican II.[3] What follows is a brief description of Bishop Fiordelli's contributions that illustrate how he tried, especially in debates on what came to be no. 11 of the Dogmatic Constitution on the Church, to promote a conception of family life that had become obscured for many Catholics.

(a) The first intervention

At the Thirty-Fourth General Congregation (5 December 1962), four days after the introduction by Cardinal Ottaviani to the council fathers of the first draft 'On the Church', Bishop Pietro Fiordelli was given permission to speak. The first annual session of the council was fast coming to an end; only two more days of speeches were scheduled. Cardinal Alfrink was presiding, and noon was fast approaching, at which time the seriously ailing Pope John XXIII was to appear on the balcony overlooking St Peter's Square to give his blessing. Bishop Fiordelli addressed the council fathers, arguing that a substantial section on the sacrament of marriage and the Christian family was needed. Alfrink interrupted the bishop's speech, claiming that the issue of marriage did not seem germane to the discussion at hand. Fiordelli retorted that marriage and the Christian family were indeed at the heart of church life, but agreed to summarize his written text in only a few words. In the written text, subsequently published in the *Acta*, we read for the first time the family described in these discussions as the domestic church.[4] In his ecclesiological remarks Fiordelli argued that the universal church comprised a vast number of local churches or dioceses, but that the diocese was not the last sub-division of the church. Christian families should be conceived of as *minusculae ecclesiae* (mini-churches). As proof for the antiquity of this teaching, he cited texts from St John Chrysostom and St Augustine that described the family as a small church or as a domestic church.

(b) The written submission (early 1963)

Fiordelli followed up this interrupted speech with a carefully written submission that pleaded for a more comprehensive presentation on Christian marriage within the context of the scheme on the church.[5] He noted that the 1962 draft had a Chapter 5 on the states of evangelical perfection, but had failed to complement that teaching with a treatment on the state of Christian marriage. The passage in his written text that bears specifically on our study reads as follows:

> Therefore, following the example of the Fathers, we can call the Christian family a minuscule church expressing the mystery of the unity of Christ with the Church (cf. Eph. 5.32).

As patristic sources for this teaching he appealed to the same passages in St John Chrysostom and St Augustine that he had cited in 1962. It is interesting to note that here and in his later oral intervention Bishop Fiordelli preferred, when describing the family, the expression *minuscula ecclesia* to *domestica ecclesia*, although the council ultimately settled upon the latter expression.

(c) Direct intervention at the Second Session of Vatican II

When the second session of Vatican II convened on 29 September 1963, the Council Fathers had available to them a new draft on the church that reflected a much desired major shift in emphasis. By 1 October, the second day of the discussions (Thirty-Eighth General Congregation), the new draft 'On the Nature of the Church' was accepted as a basis of discussion. This draft is also reproduced in the Acta under the title: *Disceptatio: Schema constitutionis dogmaticae de Ecclesia*.[6] The organization of its various chapters still differed notably from the order ultimately adopted for *Lumen gentium*. For instance, Chapter 1 of the draft discusses the mystery of the church; Chapter 2 the hierarchical constitution of the church and specifically the episcopate; Chapter 3 the people of God and especially the laity. As is well known, the order of Chapters 2 and 3 was ultimately reversed in the final text.

The reference to the family as a 'domestic church' at this stage was contained in the draft under no. 24: 'The universal priesthood, the *sensus fidei* and charisms of the faithful'. The section included a curious passage about the role of the family and the parents' ecclesial tasks, a passage that was dropped in the final version. Describing the parents' role in handing on the Christian faith, the draft stated: *'In hac velut Ecclesia domestica, parentes saepe sunt primi fidei praecones, quasi munus episcopale, ut ait Augustinus, exercent, et sacras etiam vocationes Deo dante fovent.'*[7] [In what might be called domestic church, parents are often the first preachers of the faith, exercise a sort of episcopal function, as Augustine says, and foster sacred vocations which God deems fit to bestow.]

The draft passage provided several references from St Augustine as well as from other Latin and Greek fathers about the role of the parents, especially that of the father. The particular text of Augustine that appears to be the basis of the claim that parents exercise within the family a *munus episcopale* is Augustine's comment in *Serm.* 94 (*PL* 38, 580ff.) where he urges the *paterfamilias*: *'Agite vicem nostram in domibus vestris. Episcopus inde appelatus est, quia superintendit, quia intendendo curat.'*[8] [Take our place in your homes. The head of a family is therefore called a 'bishop' because he exercises supervision and because he provides care by listening.]

Bishop Fiordelli once again addressed the council fathers during the Fiftieth General Congregation (17 October 1963).[9] Some of the same themes mentioned in his earlier written text were repeated. He was one of seventeen speakers who spoke that day on various issues related to what was then the schema's Chapter 3 on 'the people of God and especially the laity.' Ultimately, as is generally known, it was decided to divide the material into two separate chapters, one of which became Chapter II ('The People of God') and another Chapter IV ('The Laity'). Fiordelli gave an eloquent defence of Roman Catholicism's need to stress local or particular churches by using a formula that was adopted almost verbatim in the definitive text of the Dogmatic Constitution on the Church: *'Ecclesia vero universalis articulatur in ecclesias particulares . . . '* [In fact, the universal Church is expressed in particular churches]. He commented on the relationship of the Church to the family by saying: *'Unde, exemplum SS. Patrum secuti, tum ex Oriente tum ex Occidente, iuremerito, uti innuit schema, familiam christianam veluti parvam ecclesiam vocare possumus et debemus, in se habentem communicationem mysterii unitatis et amoris inter Christum et Ecclesiam.'* [Hence following the example of the fathers of both the East and the West, we can and should describe the Christian family, as the draft correctly states, as a sort of small church expressing the mystery of unity and love between Christ and the church.] He then urged the council fathers to include as a footnote a citation that calls the family household a church. The text he ascribed to St Augustine, but in fact it is a citation from St John Chrysostom.

In his intervention, Bishop Fiordelli expressed reservations about ascribing a *munus episcopale*, 'episcopal responsibility', to parents. Apparently his misgivings were shared by others, since the expression was eventually dropped from the conciliar draft. He also took exception to the phrase '*in hac veluti* **domestica Ecclesia**', which nonetheless was retained in the final text despite his objections. He argued: 'The idea is a good one, but the expression, apparently Pauline, although Paul is not cited, had its own proper historical context which is altogether different from the treatment of matrimony here under discussion. Therefore, instead of "domestic church" we should say "small church", as do the fathers.' Bishop Fiordelli's preference for the term 'small church' was based on the usage found in St John Chrysostom, who in several places associates the family household (*oikia*) with the 'small church' (*ekklesia mikra*) (cf. *PG* 62, 143; *PG* 62, 549).

(d) The final text

During the Third Session of Vatican II (Eighty-Second General Congregation, 17 September 1964, and the Eighty-Third General Congregation, 18 September 1964, voting took place on those revised sections of the draft text on the church which now corresponds with the final nos. 9–12 of *Lumen gentium*. The definitive text of the Constitution on the Church refers to the role of parents in the family and calls the family a 'domestic church' in no. 11:

> *In hac velut* **Ecclesia domestica** *parentes verbo et exemplo sint pro filiis suis primi fidei praecones, et vocationem unicuique propriam, sacram vero peculari cura, foveant oportet.*

Among the several English translations of this passage available, the best in my judgment is the one published in Norman Tanner's two-volume edition of the ecumenical councils.

> The [family] is, as it were, the domestic church in which the parents must be for their children, by word and by example, the first preachers

of the faith; encouraging each in her or his vocation and paying special attention to a sacred vocation.

What the drafters understood by a 'sacred vocation' is what we would refer to as a vocation to the priesthood or to religious life, as other English translations make clear. A vocation is to be fostered 'with special care if it be to religion' (Flannery) or 'fostering with special care any religious vocation' (Abbott).

Although no footnote is given in this section to specific patristic references, it is clear from the *Acta* that the drafters of the text had in mind passages cited in 1962 by Fiordelli such as St John Chrysostom, *PG* 54, 607, *In Gen.* ch. 6, para. 2, which reads *ekklesian poieson sou ten oikian* [Make your home a church], and St Augustine, *PL* 40, 450: *De bono viduitatis*, no. 29: '*Deinde obsecro vos per illum a quo et hoc donum acceptistis, et hujus doni praemia speratis, ut me quoque orationibus vestris memineritis inserere cum tota domestica vestra ecclesia.*' [I implore you, through him from whom you have received this gift, that you together with your domestic church remember to include me also in your prayers.]

The idea that the family is a domestic church is also affirmed in Vatican II's Decree on the Laity (*Apostolicam actuositatem*), no. 11, although here the family is described as a 'domestic sanctuary of the church'. The word sanctuary is meant to denote a holy place for prayer and love. 'The mission of being the primary vital cell of society has been given to the family by God himself. This mission will be accomplished if the family, by the mutual affection of its members and by family prayer, presents itself as a domestic sanctuary of the Church [*tamquam domesticum sanctuarium Ecclesiae se exhibeat*] . . . ' The Decree on the Laity is here repeating some of the very words regarding parents' responsibilities to foster children's vocations found in the Dogmatic Constitution on the Church.

This section on family life in Vatican II's statement on the laity drew upon the ordinary teaching of recent popes, especially Pius XI's encyclical *Casti connubii* (1930), numerous allocutions of Pius XII, and segments of John XXIII's encyclical *Mater et Magistra* (1961). A close analysis of the council's specific verbal borrowings from papal writings would be a useful study.

In the very same year (1962) that Bishop Fiordelli was first speaking of the family as a 'domestic church', an extensive article was published by the Paris-based Orthodox theologian Paul Evdokimov on the same topic. Whether or not Bishop Fiordelli or his theological advisors may have known about the French essay published in *Anneau d'Or: Cahiers de spiritualité conjugale et familiale* is not known, but it was a serendipitous coincidence.[10] Evdokimov's study contains additional patristic references, and concentrates more on the relationship of husband and wife than specifically on the family and the parents' interaction with their children. The two contributions complement each other effectively and show a happy symbiosis of Eastern and Western theology.

After the council, the expression 'domestic church' continues to be used often. In his post-synodal Apostolic Constitution, *Familiaris consortio* [On the Role of the Christian Family in the Modern World], Pope John Paul II summarized the work of the 1980 International Bishops' Synod on Family Life and drew upon what Vatican II had said of the family as domestic church at the same time expanding on the theme.[11]

Similarly, in preparation for the United Nations' 1994 International Year of the Family, the Bishops of the United States of America published an impressive pastoral message on 17 November 1993, entitled 'Follow the Way of Love'.[12] This pastoral encourages families to see their home as a domestic church (a teaching which, it argues, was found in 'the early church' and one which 'was under-emphasized for centuries, but reintroduced by the Second Vatican Council'). It articulates this teaching in the context of a communion ecclesiology and notes that the 'domestic church is not complete by itself, of course. It should be united with and supported by parishes and other communities within the larger church' (p.436).

The teaching of Vatican II on the family as a domestic church provided a useful counterbalance to a frequent overemphasis since the Council of Trent on marriage as a contract. It helped reappropriate the notion that the Christian couple and their children participate in an ongoing sacramental reality through which they are sanctified and invited to participate actively in the outward mission of the church, especially through service and hospitality. The challenge to today's church is to empower the ministerial potential of the family. New pastoral approaches are needed to enable families to realize their liturgical and ministerial resourcefulness.[13] Despite the theological correctness of Catholicism's reappropriation of the family as 'domestic church', the teaching is formulated in a doctrinal vacuum that fails to address serious issues that need to be articulated in dialogue with sociologists, psychologists and demographers, to name only a few. As the Catholic Church approaches the new millennium, its teachers will need to listen attentively and to discern painstakingly the signs of the times.

Notes

1. For the genesis of the Dogmatic Constitution on the Church, see Umberto Betti, OFM, 'Histoire chronologique de la Constitution', *L'Eglise de Vatican II*, ed. G. Baraúna, vol. 1, Unam Sanctam 51a, Paris 1967, 57–83.
2. Bishop Fiordelli was born in Città di Castello on 9 January 1916. He was ordained priest in 1938 and bishop in 1954. He retired from being bishop of Prato on 7 December 1991.
3. *Acta Synodalia Sacrosancti Concilii Oecumenici Vaticani II*. 5 vols. in 25 folios, plus 2 vols. appendices, 1 vol., index. Vatican City 1960–1989 (henceforth called *Acta synodalia*). The text of the original (1962) *Schema de Ecclesia* is published in *Acta synodalia*, Vol. I, pars 4, 12–121.
4. *Acta synodalia*, Vol. I, pars 4, 309–11.
5. *Acta synodalia*, Vol. II, pars 1, 794–5.
6. *Acta synodalia*, Vol. II, pars 1, 215–81.
7. *Acta synodalia*, Vol. II, pars 1, 259.
8. *Acta synodalia*, Vol. II, pars 2, 264 n.8.
9. *Acta synodalia*, Vol. II, pars 3, 21–4.
10. '*Ecclesia domestica*', *L'Anneau d'Or: Cahiers de spiritualité conjugale et familiale* 107, 1962, 353–62; reprinted in his *La Nouveauté de l'Esprit: Etudes de spiritualité*, Spiritualité orientale no. 20, Bégrolles 1977, 218–36.
11. English text in *Origins* 11, nos. 28–29 (24 December 1981), 437–68. The Latin text is found in *AAS* 74, 1982, 81–191.
12. See *Origins* 23, no. 25 (2 December 1993), 433–43.
13. Especially useful studies are: Mitch and Kathy Finley, *Christian Families in the Real World: Reflections on a Spirituality for the Domestic Church*, Chicago 1984; James B. and Kathleen McGinnis, 'Family as Domestic Church', in *One Hundred Years of Catholic Social Thought: Celebration and Challenge*, ed. John A. Coleman, SJ, Maryknoll, NY 1991, 120–34.

The Church as Family in Africa
F. Kabasele Lumbala

At the African synod in Rome, the bishops of Africa defined their form of the church as being that of a family. At the end of the first sessions the document[1] states: 'the model of this church of Africa is that of a church as communion, well expressed in an African context as the church as family of God. It is around this central idea that the proclamation of the gospel is being lived out and structured in Africa and on Madagascar. This conception of the church as family of God has its roots deep in Holy Scripture, but it also has anthropological roots in African and Malagasy cultures.'

This does not push aside the conciliar idea of the church as 'people of God', but it does emphasize the importance of the reality of the family for the African continent, as the 'place where models of ecclesial experience lived out in Africa emerge . . . This family spirit, broadened into the ecclesial community, is a solid basis for living out concretely the communion of the church as the family of God, the people gathered in the unity of the Father and of the Son and of the Holy Spirit. And this church is lived out at its base as a domestic church, and is given different names: Christian base communities, living ecclesial communities, small Christian base communities . . . the corner-stone of the edifice of the church of today and tomorrow.'[2] This is the reality which will be taken as a way of theological and catechetical development.

However, in the gospel Jesus seems to have played down these family bonds: 'Whoever loves his father and his mother more than me cannot be my disciple' (Matt. 10.27–28). 'Who is my brother, my sister, my mother? Those who do the will of God' (Luke 8.21). Jesus did not neglect his family; but he wanted to emphasize that one could not prefer one's family to the kingdom: he emphasized that when there is a conflict between these two values, the kingdom must be preferred. This is the same logic as that behind the order to cut off one's hand or pluck out one's eye if they prevent one from entering into the kingdom. When Jesus speaks of his mother (or his sisters and brothers) as the one who does the will of God, this is not to discredit Mary, but to stimulate us to see that even our family bonds are transformed in relation to the will of God and that they are orientated on doing the will of God. In other words, it is not enough to have a blood tie with someone; this blood tie must also be the place where the gospel is proclaimed.

The family was an important reality in yesterday's Africa, as it is in that of today, since our societies are essentially based on marriage, community and solidarity. Certainly today the modern cities of Black Africa have created new networks of relationships, professional relationships, neighbourliness and religious relationships. But it is interesting to note how these new relationships are woven on the family pattern. It is as if through these new networks of relationships Africans were indefatigably pursuing and recovering the family relationship. Thus for example in work places there will be the 'older ones' (big brothers and big sisters) and the 'younger ones' (little brothers and little sisters), 'fathers' and 'mothers' and 'children', depending on age group, who meet on a factory floor, in a workshop or an office. It is no coincidence that in our local Christian communities one again finds the 'older ones' in the church, and that these are not addressed as 'Mr' or 'Mrs' but rather as 'father' or 'mother'. In most of these communities the diocesan priest is called 'Father'.

Even when Africans live far from their kinsfolk, they preserve an important range of references to their family and their ancestors. In 1983 a Zairean religious, now a nun who has taken perpetual vows, had been cited for having instigated a rebellion among the young religious. This was against a traditionalist spiritual director who had been completely overtaken by the reforms of the council and was forcing the sisters still to wear the white European habit, regarding the African loincloth as 'prostitute's dress'. It had been decided that she should be dismissed, and one of the members of the council had warned her of this. The evening before she was due to appear before the council, she confided the matter to her dead father, saying, 'My father, you know the sincerity which led me to stir up the others against this old-fashioned goat and which has led us to the brink . . . do something up there, intervene in this affair.' The convocation was delayed because the Superior and the Father had to travel . . . and then it was definitively annulled.

Several years later, on the day when she was to fly to Brussels, about five hours before going to the airport she had her bag, containing her passport, Belgian money, references, and plane ticket stolen on the main street of the capital. She burst into tears and thought hard of her dead father, saying, 'Father, don't go to sleep.' She retraced her steps going through all the shops she had entered. About half an hour later, in front of one of the shops, she saw a crowd and some religious approaching in a car. Seeing the religious, a man shouted to them, 'Hey, sisters, a religious has been the victim of a theft. The picture on the passport and the identity card show that she's a religious. Will you take this bag to the convent?' The religious saw that it was indeed their sister's bag, which had been lost an hour and a half previously.

An African priest, studying in France, wanted to get one of his sisters, who was very sick, over for medical care. She was suffering from loss of voice. But there were always obstacles in the way. One night he had a vivid dream of his dead mother and told her all about it. The next morning he went to see a French priest who without hesitation agreed to produce a document, which was a key to sorting out the matter. This was in 1985.

Serge, a famous footballer from the Ivory Coast, aged twenty-three, a former captain of the national team, had just signed a two-and-a-half year contract with a major Madrid club. He was interviewed on Radio France Internationale, on the sports programme 'Afrique Matin', on 8 January 1994. They asked him how he responded to the good fortune which had smiled on him. Among other things, he said – I quote from memory: ' . . . I shall fight to the end to honour my ancestors and all my family and open the way to other Africans . . . I ask my family to bless me so that I have no problems here in Spain, either with the people of the country or with other players, and that everything goes well.' And the commentator, who clearly understood nothing of this philosophy of life, concluded, 'Well, Serge is asking his supporters to pray for him.'

These stories bear witness to the vividness and originality of the experience of the family and especially of ancestors in the daily life of Africans. I have taken them from spheres which normally are quite decultured, so that we can see the persistence of this element better. The cult of ancestors is evolving, like all cultural elements; for example, it is changing in form depending on circumstances and socio-economic structures. But the basis remains. And that is what is important for our churches in Africa, as an incontestable fact which has to be integrated into the organizational structures and the life of the church there.

One of the great attempts to integrate family structure has been in the Christian rites and celebrations in Black Africa. Pastor Mnyagwata Willy in Zimbabwe associates 'elders by blood' with the Christian reconciliation of two belligerents.[3] Almost all the African eucharistic prayers contain a mention of ancestors who are invoked or linked with the prayer of the community.[4]

Relgious professions and priestly ordinations have given an important role to the candidate's family during the celebration.[5] Thus for example in ordination, during the call of the candidate, the family will speak, to bless their child and give him his alb. Here is an extract from a ritual of Kasayi (one of the ecclesiastical provinces of Zaire):

> At the beginning, at the moment when the bishop asks whether the candidates are worthy, the priest presenting them replies:
>
> 'According to the opinion of those who have followed them during their formation, we think that they are worthy. But their parents are here. Let them also be heard on this question, since the shoulders are never higher than the neck.'
>
> The bishop turns towards the parents and asks if they have anything to say, and if they truly give their child with all their heart. They speak, showing their joy, declaring their commitment alongside that of their child, and asking the church to take care of him, in terms like this:
>
> 'This man is our blood. His commitment is also ours. With all our heart we give him to the church. We will be at his side. But see that you give him good working conditions, surround him with affection and concern. We have done our work; now you do yours.'
>
> Then turning towards their son, his parents give him the alb, saying:
>
> 'The insect which destroys the bean lies within. We who have brought you into the world will never betray you. We shall continue to fight by your side. Here is your alb; we are with you.'
>
> Then they put a bit of white kaolin on his forehead. The priest ends this first part by saying, 'We choose them for the rank of priest', and the whole assembly applauds.

This image of the church as family includes demands which go further than might appear at first sight. For example, will the point be reached when customary marriage is accepted into the life of Christians without those who are married in such a way being regarded as concubines, as is still the case? For families based on customary right are the only ones which enjoy social esteem. If a couple simply undergo a religious marriage they are not considered 'married'. The church as family must take steps to recognize the structures which safeguard families.

Another step has to be taken to meet the demands of this family ecclesiology, in relation to the way of life of African priests. In a church family, the one in charge of the local Christian community must be a married man, the father of a family. Otherwise he is still an official who has come to spend some time in a place. In our African cultures, the role of chief and elder calls for marital experience, which brings important psychological resources to the responsibility of leading a human group. It is enough to see how celibates are treated in our traditions: they are children, regardless of their age. Certainly there are African traditions which call for sexual continence. But this is always for a given period, for a particular ritual duration, never as a permanent state of life. The experience of human sexuality is no less important in communion with the creator and solidarity with one's origins. It is not by chance that the dead person who has no offspring does not have the status of a Bantu 'ancestor', the symbols of the radiance of life.

This does not condemn the celibate religious and priests in Africa. In line with certain of our African traditions, it is well understood that some people abstain from all sexual relationships, and even from all relationships with ordinary common life, in order to keep vigil for an important event (war, a journey, a meeting). The religious in Africa form part of those who put themselves in quarantine for the triumph of the kingdom. But they are not the ones who lead communities of Christians. In conformity with our cultures this role of chief and elder must be played by married men, priests. Religious who are priests could not therefore be parish priests. They can only be possible sources of inspiration, to whom appeal is made for certain specific tasks.

This should not in any case weaken the commitment of numerous diocesan priests who are celibates by office and by the present structure. They will pursue their commitments in fidelity to the word that they have given, thinking that in celibacy they have made the necessary choice, the choice of faith and the kingdom, in a framework given by the terms that an organizational structure provided for them. For if the choice is presented as being exclusively between 'marrying' and 'serving the cause of the kingdom in the priesthood', the believer who is truly called to the priestly ministry will opt for the cause of the kingdom. But that must not prevent him from thinking that other organizational structures could be created, in particular in churches which are seeking their way as in Africa, structures and modes of life in conformity both to the gospel and to the depths of African life.

Thus the concept of the church as family points the way for the churches of Africa. But at the same time it is a profound representation of African life, in which societies are firmly attached to the values of marriage, and concerned to keep these ties of blood. That represents a conception of the world and of life as a place of interaction in which beings are in vital communion. From this we can see how Black Africa in its church structures is linking up with its deepest roots and its conception of the world. And here a challenge is emerging: Black Africa will be deeply evangelized only by an evangelization of families and blood ties; that is, by leading them to find consolidation in fulfilling the will of God. Here the concept of the church as family can play the role of a catalyst.

Translated by John Bowden

Notes

1. *Synod of Bishops. Special Synod for Africa, Report of the Commissions*, Vatican City 1994, 5.
2. Ibid., 24.
3. Mnyagwata Willy, 'Inculturating the Reconciliation Experience', in *Spearhead* 92, 1986, 31.
4. Cf. the dossier published by CRTM, Paris, *A travers le monde célébrations de l'eucharistie*, Paris 1981; E. Uzukwu, *Liturgy, Truly Christian, Truly African*, Nairobi 1982.
5. Cf. my *Alliance avec le Christ en Afrique*, Athens 1987, 287–94.

Building a Spirituality of Family Life
Márcio Fabri dos Anjos

In undertaking a study of this subject, it is important to bear in mind the need to come as close as possible to a spirituality of the real situations in which families find themselves. This at least represents an attempt at avoiding an idealism that easily makes spirituality slip over into spiritualization. But this is not so simple, since the reality of family life implies a whole host of varied experiences.

There is, on the one hand, a social dimension, consisting of cultures, networks of economic and political relationships; on the other hand, family life embraces an evolution spanning the beginning and end of the lives of its members: everything that happens from birth to death – birth, childhood, adolescence, falling in love, marriage, child-bearing, separations, solitude, widowhood, death. Beyond this, we also have to take account of the conjunctural differences to which we are subject, such as states of health or sickness, for example. We therefore find different members of the same family in very different situations, and families themselves in an enormous variety of models and situations.

Faced with such diversity, the easiest thing seems to be to devise a *spiritual discourse for family life*. This is what often happens. It consists in considering a group of persons in a particular situation and directing theological and spiritual reflections to them. Such a discourse has its value in carrying spiritual nourishment theoretically to the social and personal situation in which people actually are: in love, preparing to get married, experiencing the joys and difficulties of married life, bringing up children, and so on.

We also, however, need a *discourse on the spirituality of family life*. This implies some degree of abstraction, but has its uses in critically formulating spiritual discourse for families and their members. Spirituality becomes theological reflection and systematization. This is what I propose to undertake here, taking the utmost care not to let my discourse become too abstract.

Where to situate spirituality

Faced with such diversification and versatility of family life, we need to seek to identify its central issues and basic axes. Theological reasoning has generally come to revolve around conjugal union, which, though important, is just one aspect of family life. So, 'It is necessary to jump almost from the early centuries to the present day in order to find a spirituality of the family that is not only based on experience but critically and consciously analysed.'[1]

In seeking to broaden this outlook, it will perhaps help if we take three major dimensions of family life: the course of sexual love, including the experience of begetting and being begotten; social opening and insertion; conflictivity.

1. The course of human love

The basic anthropological experience of sexual love has a course running right through the family in its construction and evolution. The family shelters its members in the evolution of the different stages of this love: conjugal, maternal/paternal, of sons and daughters, of adolescents and young people taking their first steps outside the family. Even with new modern customs and resources, infancy and old age are two stages of life that manifest needs and require care among family members.

With its attention focussed on the marriage partners, the spirituality of family life has had less to say to sons and daughters, despite the injunction of the Fourth Commandment. Still less do we find a spirituality to accompany the experience of genitality, the ways of falling in love and finding possible sexual partners. We are more used to seeing rules for moral behaviour, many of them expressed in negative form.

Beyond this, we need to note that a basic condition of families is to exist always in relation to other persons and other families, with society at large, with its groupings, systems and structures. This experience is a decisive point in devising a spirituality of family life, since it amounts ultimately to saying that the family does not have its end in itself; it does not exist of itself, but by virtue of other relationships that extend beyond it. From what we learn from the Gospels, Jesus himself had problems with the closing-in of families in his day, in trying to put forward ideals of openness and solidarity. Modern life today presents families closed in on themselves, but also the opposite experience, of the loosening of family ties, without this implying an exact strengthening of social bonds.

2. *Spirituality in conflictivity*

Conflictivity is another dimension that runs right through the experience of family life. We are used to seeing spirituality in the form of an idealized image, and so harmonious, without conflicts. At most, it recognizes conflicts on the ethical level. But family life experiences many conflicts that are inherent in the very development of individuals and their relationships. This means that conflictivity defies spirituality especially when the ideal is not only removed from real life but becomes impossible. Idealization is built up of life or behavioural models to which people simply cannot live up.

An example of this is the question of spirituality after marital break-up, especially when this is followed by a new marriage. But it is not the only example. I know a mother who confessed to her son that she had tried to have him aborted in the third month of pregnancy. And she told him: 'It was the most desperate act of love for you. We were so poor and your father was a violent alcoholic. I wanted to save you from this hell that life was for me and your five brothers and sisters. It was God's goodness that decided otherwise, so that you could be born and live.'

As can be seen, spirituality is challenged in the midst of conflicts of various kinds. Poor families, especially, show the conflictivity of the inequality of social relationships. The lack of basic conditions for a dignified life – health, employment, education, dwelling – easily forces members of a family into conflict with one another, and the whole family into conflict with socio-religious norms.

Guidelines for a Christian family spirituality

What does spirituality ultimately consist of? Spirituality occupies a space in our human condition as beings in history seeking a meaning for our lives. We need motivations to live and act. So, 'Spirituality is the motivation that guides the projects and commitments of our lives': to talk of meaning and motivations is to talk of mysticism, of spirituality.[2] It is a work of the Spirit. This also means that before talking of a Christian spirituality of family life, we have to find space for a 'basic human' spirituality,[3] in which we discover life and give it direction in the face of its challenges, within the dynamic of its evolution and in the midst of its conflicts.

Religious communities have the task of gathering the essentials and cultivating the mysticism that (in this case) motivate family life in its various dimensions. There is unfortunately no space here to go into the cultural and religious diversity that would shed more light on the wisdom of humanity in this respect. We need, however, to inquire into where to find the most important guidelines for a spirituality of family life in the Christian sense.

The 1980 Synod on the Family, in its proposition 36, defined the spirituality of family life under six main headings: it had a sense of Creation (fecundity), of Covenant ('one flesh'), of Cross, of Resurrection; it was seen as *Sign*, and as eschatological Hope. I should like to look in a different direction to point out various guidelines.

1. *A calling to be holy*

This broad concept, though little invoked explicitly, provides the main context of Christian spirituality for family life. On the one hand it means recognizing our greatness as human beings (GS 3) in our family concerns. On the other, it evokes the condition of historicity, progressivity and even ambiguity in which we find ourselves. The dynamism of the word 'calling' thereby makes it adequate to accompany the evolution and also the mishaps of life in a family. It provides us with the inspiration for family life in all its motivations and requirements on the level of following Jesus.

2. *A wise understanding of human love*

The experience of love is something basic to experience of family life. Love need not always be romantic love, but even its absence and the tensions inherent in it show its centrality. The spirituality of family life must therefore include an interpretation of the meaning of human love as experienced in the family. The most ancient biblical traditions already show the closeness between the experience of conjugal and filial love and the experience of who God is. The family experience of love (even betrayed, as in Hosea) provides a basis for experiencing who God is: love, covenant. Experiencing God starts from the experience of family. A rereading of these texts provides precisely a spiritual reading of family life: God who is Love seals us existentially with the signs of covenant and love through family ties. So the experience of family is 'the grammar God uses to express love and faithfulness'.[4] The family is thus a sort of proclamation that we are all born from love and for love. This is to stress the importance of family bonds, in love and solidarity.

The church has gone through a long process of evolution in elaborating these concepts. From a negative view of sexuality worked out in the early centuries,[5] it has come to concentrate on procreation and the bringing-up of children as the primary ends of marriage. As we know, Vatican II (GS 47–52) legitimized a previously existing framework of thought which indicated the primacy of love over reproductive capability. In his encyclical *Humanae vitae* (n. 9), Pope Paul VI anthropologically made fecundity an adjunct of 'fully human love, that is, at once sensitive and spiritual'.

3. *Gratuitousness in the light of Christ's loving-giving*

This central axis of Christian spirituality merits a detailed application to family life. As formulated in Ephesians 5.21ff., speaking of relations between husband and wife, this exposition of love as full self-giving is put forward, in different words, as the requirement for discipleship itself. It sets out the ideal of total self-giving between husband and wife, and of both to their children. It indirectly also states the provisional nature of the family itself, called to adapt itself and even to disappear, for the sake of its members and the building-up of social life.

We know that gratuitousness requires a long apprenticeship. This apprenticeship goes with the challenge to move beyond our own concerns and self-interest, so that love can be deeply 'spiritual' without ceasing to be integrally human. This aspect alone is enough to make the family the ideal model of 'domestic church'.

4. *Calling to be people of God*

This guideline for family spirituality leads us first to recover Jesus' teaching on family life, based on the experience of 'familism' of his time. This closing in of families on their interests and blood bonds led Jesus to stress the need for a break with family ties for the sake of following him. Jesus' way leads to a covenant founded on justice and solidarity, not based on ties of consanguinity. In other words, the 'people of God' is more important for Jesus than the 'family.'

At the same time, however, Jesus' teaching uses precisely the strength of family life to describe the Kingdom of God. God is Father and we are all brothers and sisters. At least in what concerns the spirituality of family life, we can recognize that the affirmation of God as Father, Son and Holy Spirit is linked in some way to the statement that we are all brothers and sisters. The Spirit teaches us to be sons and daughters with the Son; it teaches us to be brothers and sisters to one another in a covenant that extends to the shedding of blood. So the experience of family life, with the solidity of its bonds, is not rejected as something unworthy, but on the contrary is called to serve as a basic experience to be extended to all our kind: love one another as brothers and sisters. (The texts are too well known to need citing.) In this way, spirituality nourishes family life by motivating its actions in the direction of social solidarity, respect and compassion extending beyond the limits of the family itself.

Nourishing spirituality

The spirituality of family life undoubtedly has a basis in the experience of the members of families in all their diverse forms. But it is the community that is the main setting for gathering, organizing, criticizing and re-formulating this spiritual experience. In general terms, the community thereby provides the service of nourishing the spiritual meaning of family life, of choosing its most valid forms of expression, of setting out approaches and even ascetic behaviour.

The 'Christian community' can be seen existing on at least three different levels in order to provide these services: the basic family unit, family movements, and the official church. There is naturally a strong interaction among these, but the importance of each also has to be recognized.

1. *The basic family unit*

On this level, the 'Christian community' most directly gathers responses and proposals to do with the actual problems its families have to face in the complex business of daily life. It is therefore characterized by plurality, starting from actual situations. In this area, there is a powerful reworking of spiritual proposals emanating from official discourse, to the point of selecting those that appear most helpful and according less importance to those seen as unachievable. Families here organize their axiology and their 'spiritual codes'. Among poor families, for example, the Christian calling gains emphasis on the face of the basic needs of their members: the sacred mission of fathers is to ensure that their children do not go hungry – also to help their daughters make a 'good' marriage, in the sense of ensuring their survival.

On this level, spirituality is perceptibly rooted in local culture, as resistance and struggle to live. It would be impossible in the space of this article to describe the diversity and also the riches to be found in this sphere. All I can do is suggest questions that readers can pose on the level of family communities in their own areas: What values and spiritual references are actually guiding persons in their daily family experience? What tasks are seen to be most important and what Christian motivations underpin them?

In making value judgments, we have to recognize that Christian communities on this base level are also subject to the dominant cultural ethos, as well as being exposed to the bombardment of communications and projects put out by society at large. It is understandable that certain ambiguities will emerge in the spirituality that comes about at this level. These resist discernment and overcoming, but this sphere is nevertheless very rich in other noteworthy values. More attuned to life as it actually is, spirituality on this level can more rapidly penetrate into the difficulties, conflicts and very failures of family life. Less bound to a 'spiritual theory', it shows an agility in reinventing Christian spirituality in places the ideal formulas upheld by family movements and by the official Church itself have difficulty in reaching.

As examples of reinventing the spirituality of family life, I would give that of the experience of 'single mothers' in families that have broken up, with or without a new marriage, or that of the attempts to find a new balance between sexuality and fecundity in today's conditions. These represent a spirituality that accepts conflicts and failures more realistically. If we accept these circumstances as given facts, we shall more readily be able to see qualities such as welcoming, understanding and the urge to get on with life as having a Christian inspiration. This is not to downgrade the official criteria set out by the church, but an attempt to perceive the *sensus fidelium* working out a spirituality for the actual and possible experiences of themselves, the faithful.

2. *Family movements*

The spirituality of family life shows other aspects when viewed from movements devoted to it. Here one has to consider the nature of the 'movement' itself: what social dimensions or social classes it takes in, what aspects of family life it concentrates on, and at the same time what type of spirituality it proposes. In fact, many such 'family movements' are 'trans-regional', are made up of middle-class members and have their own spiritual concerns limited by statute. They generally lay great stress on conjugal harmony and the upbringing of children. Among the poor of the

Third World, however, other types can be found. These are family movements that struggle for survival or for basic needs, such as those of landless peasants, or *favela*-dwellers. The thrust of their spirituality is in such cases inevitably slanted more in the direction of valuing solidarity and mutual help. But then, curiously, they are no longer called 'family movements'. Again it is up to readers to find out: What family movements are active in your area, and what spiritual lines do they follow to encourage Christian life? And what are the most important challenges they seek to respond to?

In making an even generic evaluation of such movements, it would seem to be important to recognize, on the one hand, the service they render in forming and nourishing a spirituality of family life. They have a power to bring people together; they provide an area for participation and communication for individual families in their spiritual experience; they keep close to some specific problems that affect families. On the other hand, they have their problematical aspects. Among these is a 'familism' restricted to the narrow world of family problems alone, lacking a dimension of openness beyond the family; at times this closing-in is brought about by narrowing the movement's outlook to the classes of family envisaged by its membership. The trans-regional nature of such movements can also often give rise to problems of insertion in and commitment to local communities.

3. *The official church*

By this level is understood the spirituality formulated by theologians and the *magisterium* – and also by the clergy. There is no doubting the necessary and valuable quality of the discourse of the *magisterium*, marked by its concern for the great Christian referents of a family spirituality, by ideal proposals and common criteria by which to pattern Christian family life. Marked too by the task of delineating the institutional identity, it seeks universality in its proposals, guards a line of tradition, and seeks a complete doctrinal formulation.[6]

The most significant difficulty on the level of the spirituality officially proposed resides perhaps in the fact of its being marked by ideal requirements. The very model of family on the basis of which pronouncements are made is an ideal family. As Pope John Paul II has recognized, this supposes a basic spiritual difficulty for 'very many people who cannot relate in any way to what might properly be defined as a family'; these are precisely those 'large sectors of humanity [who] live in conditions of enormous poverty.'[7] In other words, we end up recognizing that, precisely for the very poorest, we have no spiritual word to encourage and dignify them as sons and daughters of God.

The question is complex, because the institution needs an institutional model that can symbolize and express the ideal it puts forward. But what is functional in terms of the institution can be impractical in terms of spirituality. This happens when the ideal model is brought in as a measure of the real, which includes weakness and failure. Faced with marital problems and breakdown, there is no denying the attempt to offer 'means of salvation'.[8] But some ask themselves how far we are succeeding in giving more space to mercy and in not confusing the criterion of love with that of perfection.[9]

These are not questions that can be resolved easily. At the same time, however, the community runs the risk of losing the signs of the Spirit coming from the underside of history, of failing to recognize and support the deep charcteristics of unselfishness seen, for example, in 'single mothers' constantly and heroically devoting themselves to their children, or in couples and families setting out once more on the trail of fidelity in unofficial moulds. As a community we must not presume to take in every situation, nor to be able to organize all faith experiences in their different contexts. We must not repeat the experience of the synagogue in the time of Jesus, when, in its zeal for the faith of the Israelites, it ended by discriminating against the poor who could not live up to its parameters of perfection.

Perspectives and tasks for the future

The spirituality of family life faces a disturbing question precisely in the changes launching us at high speed into the future. What spiritual motivations can we provide for family life at a time when this is changing in its innermost relationships? Thinking of families in this projection of future that to a great extent is already in our midst, I should like to put forward three basic tasks, seen from a Christian viewpoint.

1. To rediscover love as gratuitousness

If spirituality is to be set on the level of Christian motivations, there is no hiding the fact that other 'spiritualities' are constantly on offer as inspiration for new forms of family life. One obvious tendency today is the affirmation of subjectivity, of an individualistic stamp. Individual interests play an important role in defining actions and attitudes. Besides this, the organization of society itself, under the impulse of new means of production, has greatly alleviated the burden we bear for one another. In a way, we are conveniently 'third-partying' the cares previously taken on individually, in inter-personal relationships.

The effects of this on family life are clear. The very word 'love' is undergoing a sequestration, coming to mean simply the sexual act. We are looking to third parties to take on the care of sick relatives, of elderly parents, of small children. We are even coming to the extreme of using the womb as a third party for bearing children.

These observations are not designed to be taken as a radical criticism of the organization of social services, nor as a condemnation of the techno-scientific advances of modern living. They are rather an attempt to set out some pointers to indicate that there are great changes taking place that affect even the way we love. The fact is that in a society which sharpens competitiveness as the spring of relationships, and at the same time sells resources for avoiding effort and work, we need to rediscover forms of loving gratuitously and spaces in which to do so.

2. *Reinventing fertility*

Fertility, in the field of human reproduction, has become the field of numerous ethical prohibitions that impinge on the spirituality of family life. Science has devised means of separating biological fertility completely from sexual love. It has in practice given love autonomy with regard to fertility. At the same time, the 'social cost' of having children has increased. And demographic alarms are sounding, telling us that reducing the number of children is beginning to be a pressing responsibility.

Without going into the ethical ambiguities presented by the subject, it seems important to produce a somewhat better evaluation, from the angle of spirituality, of the challenge Christian families find themselves facing. On the one hand, they are faced with a very strong anti-conceptive and abortionist mentality in society at large. And on the other, at the same time they are faced with the need to engineer some control of births, with the necessary intensification of the bonds of love. The concerns of the church have focussed enough on the question of the means of achieving this. One possible way out might be found through further developing the concept that Vatican II (AA, 11) mentioned as 'fertility in the broad sense'.

3. *Increasing solidarity*

The spirituality of family life will, in my view, increasingly develop alongside the demands of social solidarity. The political and economic systems ruling our society allow us to speak openly, without apology, of those who are 'excluded'. The gulf between some families and others, some children and others, the included and the excluded, those who have a chance in society and those who have none, is growing steadily wider.

How can Christian spirituality fail to react in the face of such facts, which society itself is at pains to make clear? The tasks stemming from this situation are arduous and for the moment undefined. Solidarity with excluded families, required if we are to go to the roots of the problem, means that we must either correct the present system or devise alternatives to it.

These are huge tasks, which would leave us bewildered if we had to face them alone. But freeing the unselfishness locked up in the hearts of the poor and contradicted by the individualist mentality – this is something that can be accomplished by the Holy Spirit working in us.

Translated by Paul Burns

Notes

1. See G. Campanini, 'Familia', in S. Fiores and T. Goffi (eds.), *Dicionário de Espiritualidade*, São Paulo 1989, 436.
2. S. Galilea, *El Camino de la espiritualidad*, Bogotá 1985, 26; P. Casaldáliga and J.-M. Vigil, *The Spirituality of Liberation*, Maryknoll, NY and Tunbridge Wells 1994, 2–5.
3. Ibid., 13–14.
4. W. Kasper, *The Theology of Marriage*, São Paulo 1990, 58.
5. P. Brown, *The Body and Society: Men, Women and Sexual Renunciation in Early Christianity*, New York and London 1988.
6. The major papal documents are: Leo XIII, *Arcanum illud*, 1880; Pius XI, *Casti connubii*, 1930; Paul VI, *Humanae vitae*, 1968; John Paul II, *Familiaris consortio*; see also *Gaudium et spes*, 47-52.
7. *Familiaris consortio*, 85.
8. Ibid., 84; cf. *Humanae vitae*, 25.
9. 'Western culture has taken love as a fundamental reference. But love loves only what is good. What is evil is not loved. Love implies a demand that is at once its grandeur and its limitation: it wants the other to be perfect in order to love him/her without reserve,' J.-M. Huguenin, 'L'Eglise de la miséricorde', *Teresianum* 44, 1993, 281.

Family Values and Ideals
Marciano Vidal

In this article I propose to analyse the moral foundation of the family, that is, the values and ideals that govern family life to make it wholesome and enriching for both family members and society in general.

In order to formulate the question precisely, we must remember that the family has existed and exists today in various forms. This family variety, both in the past and today, gives rise to different ethical rules for family life, both in fact and in theory. One of the factors defining the family model is its ethos: whether the family is traditional, nuclear or post-nuclear.

In this article I want to consider the family as such, rather than the various different family models; I want to consider the family as a universal human reality, over and above historical and cultural variations. I realize that this abstract general approach may lead to fallacies about the family, but I also believe that it is possible to set out some 'minimum ethical rules' by which different existing and historical family models can be judged.

I shall consider these ethical guidelines under four headings, corresponding to fundamental aspects of the family: its reasons for existing, its purpose, its present situation, the way in which it is Christian.

1. The reason the institution of the family exists

First and foremost, the family is a human institution, which is both 'natural' and 'cultural'. As an institution, it is given certain functions, which are usually divided into universal functions (breeding and upbringing of children) and changing ones (economic, cultural, religious, etc).

Regarded as an institution, the family exists to serve certain values and ideals. What is the moral foundation of the institution of the family?

In the world today the family's changing functions have varied a great deal. Some have lost importance (for example, its economic functions: the family is not a social unit for production, but for consumption). All these functions have changed (in their purpose, influence and intensity). The family's universal functions are also subject to socio-cultural variations. Consider, for example, the new understanding and experience of sexuality, the reduction in its procreative function, and the new reproductive technology, etc.

What has not changed is the family's reason for existing, which is its humanizing function. The Second Vatican Council noted this function at the beginning of its treatise on marriage and the family: 'The well-being of each person and of human and Christian society is strictly linked to the prosperity of the conjugal and family community'.[1]

In the world today, the family's humanizing function is displayed in two ways: it is personalizing and it is socializing. I believe that this is where the institution of the family proves its positive value now. I also believe that the recent documents of the church's magisterium on the family should be set in this personalizing and socializing context.

(a) Personalizing power

The institution of the family is the proper environment for the formation of the human person. This personalizing function takes place in the family through the following processes:

– The family helps to integrate the 'I' and thus shapes the whole personality of the human individual. 'Indeed, the presence and influence of the different and complementary models of father and mother (masculine and feminine); the bond of mutual affection; the atmosphere of trust, intimacy, respect and freedom; the framework of social life within a natural hierarchy – mellowed by this family atmosphere – all help the family to form strong and balanced personalities for society.'[2]

– The family develops channels for genuine interpersonal relations, through which emotional stability can be attained. 'Relationships between family members are inspired and guided by the law of "gratuity". This means that each and every family member is accorded a personal dignity with unique value. The family becomes a place of cordial welcome, meeting and conversation, of generosity and disinterested service and deep solidarity.'[3]

– The family initiates its members into human wisdom, leading to humanism and a particular way of looking at life. The family is 'the school for the richest humanism';[4] in it 'different generations come together and help each other to attain greater wisdom'.[5]

(b) Socializing power

The family's personalizing function should not be understood as a privatized one. On the contrary, personality in the family only attains its full meaning within the socializing power of the family institution. 'The promotion of a genuine and mature communion of persons in the family becomes the first and irreplaceable school for society.'[6]

The family's socializing function works as follows:

– It acts as an example and encouragement to develop a system of social values based on the 'family atmosphere', that is, respect, dialogue, love.

– It counters the depersonalizing power of mass society. 'In the face of a society which is becoming ever more depersonalized and "massified", hence inhuman and dehumanizing – leading to the negative effects of so many forms of "evasion", such as, for example, alcoholism, drugs and even terrorism – the family still possesses and communicates tremendous energy, which can save people from anonymity, keep them aware of their personal dignity, enrich them with deep humanity and weave each unique person into the social web.'[7]

– It offers a view of life which is critical of social injustices, and thus equips people with attitudes to transform society.

The family's double function of personalization and socialization gives it its inestimable value today. Vatican II, Pope Paul VI and John Paul II all agree upon this humanizing vision of the family. Each adopts the quotation: 'The family constitutes the natural place and most effective instrument for humanizing and personalizing society. The family collaborates in an original and profound way in constructing the world, making possible a properly human life. In particular, it guards and transmits virtues and "values". As the Second Vatican Council says, in the family different generations come together and help each other to attain greater wisdom and to create harmony between personal rights and the other demands of social life.'[8]

2. The purpose of the family

Corresponding to what the family 'is', we have what the family 'does'. The family's purpose gives rise to a further set of values and ideals, which I shall consider in this second part of the article.

The encyclical *Familiaris consortio* sets out the purpose of the family under four general headings:[9]

– the formation of a community of persons;

– service to life;

— sharing in the development of society;
— sharing in the church's life and mission.

Within the limits of this article, I shall confine myself to considering the first and third of the above headings. The second (service to life) is implicit in them and the fourth belongs to the study of the family within the church.

(a) Formation of a community of persons

The family is defined by interpersonal relationships. It is made up of a 'set of interpersonal relationships — the marriage relationship, and that of father, mother, son and daughter, sister, brother — through which each human person is introduced into the "human family"'.[10]

Interpersonal relationships in the family make it a community of persons: 'The family, which is created by love, is a community of persons: wife and husband, parents and children, other relations.'[11] Hence communion is the family way of life: 'the law of married love is communion and sharing, not domination', and the family's ultimate aim is 'really to become a centre of communion and sharing'.[12]

The family becomes the special place for communion and sharing in the following ways:

— It makes love the principle of communion: 'Without love, the family cannot live or grow as a family of persons.'[13] 'Love, which permeates the interpersonal relationships of the different family members, is the inner energy shaping and giving life to the family communion and community.'[14]

— Love in action leads to the development of persons. The family is a 'maker of persons' (Medellín). 'Because the family is and should always be a communion and community of persons, love is what gives it its strength to acknowledge, respect and encourage each of its members in the highest dignity of personhood . . . The moral criterion for the authenticity of conjugal and family relationships consists in the promotion of the dignity and vocation of each person, who attains his or her fulfilment through the genuine gift of self.'[15]

— Family life creates opportunities for rich interpersonal communion:

through acts of free generosity;
through permanent willingness to make up quarrels: the family communion 'requires a ready and generous willingness on the part of all to be understanding and tolerant, to forgive and make up quarrels';[16]
through acts of respect and encouragement for personal individuality: the family communion accepts and encourages each member 'as a new, individual, unique and unrepeatable person'.[17]

– It favours effective forms of sharing. For this, a family structure is required that is (a) democratic (as opposed to authoritarian); (b) equal (as opposed to dominated by paternalism and machismo); (c) responsible (as opposed to being based on authority and obedience).

(b) Sharing in the development of society

If the family is really a place for communion and sharing, it also becomes a 'promoter of human development' (Medellín). 'Communion and sharing daily in the home, in moments of joy and difficulty, represent the most effective way of teaching children to become active, responsible and fruitful members of the wider society.'[18]

As well as coining a happy phrase, Vatican II made an important point when it stated that 'the family is the richest school of humanism'.[19] Humanity is created in the family. It distils the wisdom of what is human; it inculcates the vital syntheses which make up the 'foundation of society'.[20]

In order for the family to become a school for humanism and good social behaviour, family life must be based on the following values:

– the sense of true justice, leading to respect for the personal dignity of every human person;

– the sense of real love, experienced as genuine caring and disinterested service of others, especially those who are poorer or more needy;

– self-giving, as the law which enriches family relationships and is the necessary way to learn how to serve society, knowing that it is better to give than to receive;

– the creation of conscientious persons, ready to criticize and converse in order to become aware of, oppose, denounce and seek solutions for social injustices;

– a preference for being rather than having, such as wanting power or knowledge more for its own sake rather than for the sake of serving others better.

The formation of a community of persons and sharing in the development of society are the two fundamental tasks of the family today. Thus the family offers a 'service to life',[21] in the broadest sense. At the same time it shares 'in the church's life and mission'.[22]

3. Response to the particular challenges of the present situation

Following our reflection on what the family is and does, we must now pass on to consider the present situation. What values and ideals should we stress for the family in its present situation?

(a) The challenges of the present situation
According to accepted analyses, we can state that at least in Western countries, we are confronting a profound historical change in the way the institution of the family is understood and operates.

The 'values' governing the universal significance of the institution of the family. The family is sustained by values which give it 'significance' (internal and external). There are universal values: personal fulfilment, development of emotional maturity and sexuality, parents' desire to influence their children, integration via the family into the broader network of social relations. However, important changes are taking place in the way these values are understood and being implemented:

(i) The change in the concept of sexuality, which is no longer identified with procreation, but seen as an exercise of personal freedom.

(ii) The change in the understanding of the relationship between the individual and society. As opposed to the 'communitarianism' of the past, we see the appearance of 'individualism' as a requirement for personal fulfilment.

(iii) The change that has taken place in the manner of understanding and experiencing personal happiness. It is a 'short-term' goal, and carries no concomitant asceticism or renunciation. It is measured by realistic parameters, without regard for meta-individual and meta-historical rewards.

The structure of the family as a 'institution'. The changes here are the ones which most obviously change the family 'model'. The following factors have contributed to this change:

(i) Marriage, as the institutional origin of the family, has moved towards the pole of freedom and individualism. From marriage of convenience or by 'arrangement' between families, we have moved towards marriage as an alliance, to marriage as a personal bond, and thence to marriage purely by consent.

(ii) The purely consensual form of marriage (cohabitation, free unions) gives rise to a new family model: a non-matrimonial family.

(iii) The introduction of divorce gives rise to new forms of household: single-person households; aggregate families, including children of previous marriages (multi-parent households).

(iv) Side by side with marriage and free unions between heterosexual couples we find other forms, such as unions between homosexuals, some of which may create a family by means of reproduction technology.

Family functions and life cycle. Here there are many changes with very concrete results. I will limit myself to mentioning only two factors as signs of change:

(i) Family relationships are becoming more equal (with the downgrading of machismo and the raising of women's consciousness); and more democratic (through the decrease in parental authoritarianism and acceptance of children's rights).

(ii) Childbearing takes place more responsibly (by 'freely chosen' pregnancies, which are not 'blindly' accepted). As well as the low fertility rate, we should mention the fact that some couples, whether married or not, decide not to have any children and become 'childless families'. Side by side with marriage, we have teenage pregnancies, pregnancy in single mothers (one-parent households), and pregnancy through reproductive tehcnology in 'virgins', who want to be mothers without getting married or having sexual relations.

(b) The ethical response to the new challenges

We need moral discernment to guide us in the new situations arising in the family of today. By way of example, I should like to refer to three values, which in my view need to be reformulated to respond to these challenges:

Understanding of human sexuality. The Augustinian view persists of sexuality and its role within marriage and the family. It is based on a certain pessimism about humanity, the stress on continence as the ethical and religious way to overcome lust, an excessive linking of sexuality to procreation. We must moderate this Augustinian trend through other theological insights, not based on the Augustinian view of humanity. Only thus can we offer a fully positive and balanced Christian view of marriage and the family.

Clear interpretion of the principle of 'responsible childbearing'.

Sometimes certain well-intentioned and correctly formulated family policies come up against a muddled interpretation of the Catholic doctrine of procreation.

Neither totalitarian social power nor irresponsibility on the part of the couple are compatible with the responsible exercise of human procreation. On the contrary, the husband and wife's responsible attitude, together with the respectful and effective help of society, constitute the basic requirements for responsible procreation. Catholic doctrine has stressed the limits both of social intervention[23] and of the couple's responsibility.[24]

Some reductive interpretations concentrate more on the 'limits' imposed upon social intervention and forget the responsibility to society and to the world itself required from the couple in the exercise of procreation. Without forgetting the couple's personal freedom, I believe that we need to look at the ethical implications of world population trends.

Giving due worth to the institution of marriage. One of the problems that the theology of the family must face is the present crisis in the institution of marriage as originator of the family. I have already referred to various family groupings, which are different from/alternative to the conjugal family. From the stable heterosexual couple (with or without a family) to the lesbian family (through the use of reproductive technology), to single-parent families, there is a whole range of family situations which differ from the marriage-family. What response should we make to this situation in our family policy?

The general criterion is: 'The institutional value of marriage should be recognized by the public authorities; the situation of non-married couples should not be placed on a level with those who are properly married.'[25] Without placing them on the same level as conjugal families, family policy should concern itself with non-conjugal families, with particular regard to the care of their children.

4. The way in which the family is Christian

The encyclical *Familiaris consortio* proposes the preferential option for the poor as one of the criteria for understanding the Christian purpose of the family.[26]

The Christian family is open and committed to the cause of the poor. This is one of the genuinely 'Christian' features in our understanding of the family.

Hence it follows that family policies claiming to be inspired by the Christian vision of the family must reflect this preferential option for poor and marginalized families. I stress some concerns which must be paramount:

– Social policies which give effective support to families which suffer from social and cultural marginalization:[27]
  Ethnic minority families who are culturally, economically, politically and socially marginalized;
  poor families;
  families containing members who are physically or mentally handicapped;

families with members who are drug addicts, in prison, etc.;
old people who suffer human and social marginalization;
families of immigrants, refugees or exiles.

– Help for broken families, who need a series of social services in order to function as a family at a particular time. For them we need a policy of Family Centres, social services which are not manipulated by party politics, and which work with increasing professionalism.

– Special attention to those who have no family. 'Large sectors of humanity live in conditions of enormous poverty with little family help, because promiscuity, lack of housing, irregular relationships, mean that they do not have any real family. There are others who for various reasons have remained alone in the world. Nevertheless, there can be 'good news of the family' even for them.[28]

Among those with no family, we must remember children deprived of parents or abandoned by them. Family policies should make adoption easy and welcome these children with no family. Christian feeling supports adoption, seeing it as one of the expressions of the purpose of the family.[29]

Translated by Dinah Livingstone

Notes

1. *Gaudium et spes*, 47.
2. Medillín, III, IIa, 1.
3. *Familiaris consortio*, 43.
4. *Gaudium et spes*, 52.
5. Ibid., 52
6. *Familiaris consortio*, 43.
7. Ibid., 15.
8. *Familiaris consortio*, 43; the quotation is from *Gaudium et spes*, 52, and is used again by Paul VI in *Populorum progressio*, 36.
9. *Familiaris consortio*, 17–64.
10. Ibid., 15.
11. Ibid., 18.
12. *Puebla*, 582 and 568.
13. *Familiaris consortio*, 18.
14. Ibid., 21.
15. Ibid., 22.
16. Ibid., 21.
17. *Puebla*, 584.
18. *Familiaris consortio*, 37.
19. *Gaudium et spes*, 52.

20. Ibid., 52.
21. Cf. *Familiaris consortio*, 28–41.
22. Cf.ibid., 49–64.
23. *Carta de los Derechos de la Familia*, published by the Holy See (22 October 1983), art.3.
24. *Gaudium et spes*, 50.
25. *Carta de los Derechos de la Familia*, art. 1,C.
26. *Familiaris consortio*, 47.
27. *Familiaris consortio*, 41, 44, 47, 77.
28. *Familiaris consortio*, 85.
29. *Apostolicum actuositatem*, 11; *Familiaris consortio*, 41.

Contributors

CAROLYN OSIEK, RSCJ, is Professor of New Testament at Catholic Theological Union, Chicago. She is the author of *What Are They Saying about the Social Setting of the New Testament?* (1992), an editor of *Silent Voices, Sacred Lives: Women's Readings for the Liturgical Year* (1992), and co-author of a book on the family in early Christianity, forthcoming. She is book review editor of the *Catholic Biblical Quarterly*, a member of the editorial board of *The Bible Today* and *New Theology Review*, and of the advisory board of the *Journal of Early Christian Studies*. This year (1994–95), she is president of the Catholic Biblical Association of America.

Address: Catholic Theological Union, 5401 S. Cornell Ave, Chicago, Ill. 60615, USA.

CHARLES J. REID, JR, was born in Milwaukee, Wisconsin, in 1953. He graduated from the University of Wisconsin-Milwaukee in 1978, and earned JD (1982) and JCL (1985) degrees from the Catholic University of America. He earned the MA from Cornell University in 1987, and expects to receive the PhD from Cornell in December 1994. His dissertation is entitled *Rights in Thirteenth-Century Canon Law: An Historical Investigation*. He has published studies and reviews on legal history and ethics in the *Boston College Law Review*, the *St John's Law Review*, the *Michigan Law Review*, the *Cornell Law Review*, and other journals. He is the editor of *Peace in a Nuclear Age: The Bishops' Pastoral Letter in Perspective*, Washington, DC 1986. He has held the position of Lecturer in Law at the Cornell University School of Law and at present holds the position of Research Associate in Law and History at the Emory University School of Law.

Address: School of Emory University Law, Atlanta, Georgia 30322, USA.

RINUS HOUDIJK was born in Gouda, The Netherlands, in 1936. He studied theology and philosophy at the major seminary of Waarmond and later gained his doctorate under Edward Schillebeeckx at the theological faculty of Nijmegen, where he now works as a researcher. He has written various articles on ethics and moral theology in books and journals and has edited *Theologie en marginalisering*, 1992; *Om het geheim van God. Moraaltheologie in de jaren negentig*, 1993; *Dienst aan mensen*, 1995.

Address: Maasdijk 5, 5371 PD Ravenstein, The Netherlands.

F. KABASELE LUMBALA is an African priest, theologian and liturgist, professor of catechesis and liturgy in several institutions of higher education in Zaire and Europe. He has written many articles on the inculturation of Christian rites in Africa, and his books include *Alliance avec le Christ en Afrique*, Athens 1987; *Netendeleelu mujidila*, Kananga 1990, and *Symbolique bantu et symbolique chrétienne*, Kinshasa 1991.

Address: Théologat OMI, BP 8251, Kinshasa, Zaire.

SIDNEY CALLAHAN, born in Washington DC in 1933, is Professor of Psychology at Mercy College, Dobbs Ferry, New York. She has written many books and articles and is a wife and the mother of six grown children.

Address: Mercy College, Dobbs Ferry, NY 10522, USA.

GIORGIO CAMPANINI was born in 1930; he is a layman, a widower, and father of five children. He has been Professor of the History of Political Theory, teaching the sociology of the family, in the University of Parma. He now teaches at the theological faculty of Lugano and in the department of theological studies in Bologna. From his *Comunità familiare e società civile*, Brescia 1970, onwards, he has been particularly concerned with the relationship between the family and society. Recent books include *Potere politico e immagine paterna*, Milan 1985; *Realtà e problemi della famiglia contemporanea*, Milan 1989; *Le stagioni della famiglia*, Milan 1994.

Address: Via L.A. Muratori 23, 43100 Parma, Italy.

LINDA WOODHEAD is Lecturer in Christian Studies in the Department of Religious Studies, Lancaster University. She is interested in all aspects of the interaction between modernity and Christianity and her current research is in this area. She has written on Christian ethics and theology, and on contemporary manifestations of Christianity. Recent and forthcoming articles include: 'Feminism and Christian Ethics' in T. Elwes (ed.), *Women's Voices* (1992); 'Post-Christian Spiritualities', in *Religion*

(1993); and 'Communities of Goods: How Christianity Makes People Moral', in Digby Anderson (ed.), *Fear, Guilt and Shame* (1995). She is editor of *Studies in Christian Ethics*.

Address: Department of Religious Studies, Lancaster University, Lancaster LA1 4YG, England.

ENRIQUE DUSSEL was born in Argentina in 1934 and lives and teaches in Mexico. He holds doctorates in philosophy (Madrid), history (Paris) and theology (Fribourg). He has been visiting professor at Notre Dame, Union Theological Seminary, Loyola and Vanderbilt Universities. He is a founder member of EATWOT and a past president of CEHILA, as well as committee member of the Third World Theology section of *Concilium*. His many books include: *A History of the Church in Latin America. Colonialism to Liberation (1492–1979)*, Grand Rapids 1981; *History and the Theology of Liberation*, Maryknoll, NY 1976; *Ethics and the Theology of Liberation*, Maryknoll, NY 1978; *Para una Etica del la liberacion latinoamericana*, vols. I–IV, Buenos Aires-Bogota 1973–80, and later eds.; *Philosophy of Liberation*, Maryknoll, NY, and Tunbridge Wells 1988, 1993; *El ultimo Marx (1863–1882) y la liberacion latinoamericana*, Mexico City 1990; (ed.) *The Church in Latin America 1492–1992*, Tunbridge Wells and Maryknoll, NY 1992; *La Metaforas Teologicas de Marx*, Estella 1994; *Toward the Myth of Modernity: 1492*, New York 1995; *The Underside of Modernity: Apel, Ricoeur, Taylor and Rorty*, New York 1995.

Address: Celaya 21 – 402, Colonia Hipódromo, 06100 México DF, Mexico.

MARIFÉ RAMOS GONZÁLEZ was born in Madrid in 1953. She is married and has a son and a daughter. She has a degree in religious sciences from Louvain Catholic University and a degree in pastoral theology from the Pontifical University of Salamanca. For nineteen years she has taught religion in Madrid colleges (Institutos de Bachillerato). Her pastoral work is mainly concentrated on the religious education of the young and on accompanying people and groups, particularly those with addictions. She contributed to the anthology *The Voice of the Turtle Dove. New Catholic Women in Europe*, ed. Anne Brotherton (1991). She has written a number of articles on women's role in the church and society and on moral education in families. For ten years she has been on the editorial board of the journal *Religión y escuela*. She is a founder member of the 'Women and

Theology' groups and the 'Forum for Women's Studies'. She is also a member of the 'European Society of Women for Theological Research'.

Address: Fobos 17, 12a, 28030 Madrid, Spain.

NORBERT METTE was born in Barkhausen/Porta, Germany in 1946. After studying theology and sociology he gained a doctorate in theology, and since 1984 he has been Professor of Practical Theology at the University of Paderborn. He is married with three children, and is an Editorial Director of *Concilium*. He has written numerous works on pastoral theology and religious education, including: *Voraussetzungen christlicher Elementarerziehung*, Düsseldorf 1983; *Kirche auf dem Weg ins Jahr 2000* (with M. Blasberg-Kuhnke), Düsseldorf 1986; *Gemeindepraxis in Grundbegriffen* (with C. Bäumler), Munich and Düsseldorf 1987; *Auf der Seite der Unterdrückten? Theologie der Befreiung im Kontext Europas* (ed. with P. Eicher), Düsseldorf 1989; *Der Pastorale Notstand* (with O. Fuchs), Düsseldorf 1992.

Address: Liebigweg IIa, D 48165, Münster, Germany.

MICHAEL A. FAHEY, SJ, was born in 1933 and is Dean and Professor of Ecclesiology and Ecumenism in the Faculty of Theology, University of St Michael's College, Toronto, Ontario, Canada. He graduated in philosophy (Louvain) and theology (Tübingen, Dtheol, 1970). His most recent publications include 'Church', in *Systematic Theology: Roman Catholic Perspectives*, Minneapolis 1992, and *Ecumenism: A Bibliographic Overview*, Westport, CT. 1993. He has been a consultant theologian for the Orthodox/Roman Catholic Consultation in the USA since 1970.

Address: University of St Mary's College, Faculty of Theology, 81 St Mary Street, Toronto, Ontario M5S 1J4, Canada.

MÁRCIO FABRI DOS ANJOS was born in 1943 and is a Redemptorist priest. He holds a licentiate in theology from the University of São Paulo and a doctorate in theology from the Gregorianum in Rome. He has been Professor of Moral Theology at the Instituto Teologico S. Paulo since 1975, and at the Faculdade de Teologia N. S. Assunção since 1979. From 1980 to 1986 he edited *Vida Pastoral*, in São Paulo. In 1987 he was appointed director of the Alfonsianum Instituto de Teologia Moral, and in 1991 was elected President of SOTER, the Brazilian Society of Scientists of Theology and Religion. He has edited a collective volume on Moral Theology in Latin America.

Address: Instituto de Teologia Moral, rua Oliveira Alves, 164–04210 São Paulo, Brazil.

MARCIANO VIDAL was born in 1937 in San Pedro de Trones (Léon, Spain). He belongs to the Congregation of the Most Holy Redeemer. He gained his degree in theology from the Pontifical University of Salamanca, and his doctorate in moral theology from the Academica Alfonsiana (Rome). He is Ordinary Professor of Moral Theology in the Comillas Pontifical University (Madrid) and in the Higher Institute of Moral Sciences, of which he is at present the Director. He is a member of the *Concilium* editorial board. His most important publications are: *Moral y Actitudes* (4 vols.), Madrid 1990–91; *Frente al rigorismo moral, benignidad pastoral*, Madrid 1986; *La propuesta moral de Juan Pablo II*, Madrid 1994; *La familia en la vida y en la obra de Alfonso de Liguori* (1696–1787), Madrid 1995.

Address: Manuel Silvela 14, 28010 Madrid, Spain.

Members of the Advisory Committee for Moral Theology

Directors

Lisa Sowle Cahill	Chestnut Hill, MA	USA
Dietmar Mieth	Tübingen	Germany

Members

Emmanuel Agius	Qrendi	Malta
Klaus Demmer	Rome	Italy
Enrique Dussel	Mexico City	Mexico
Margaret Farley	New Haven	USA
Marcio Fabri dos Anjos	Sao Paolo	Brazil
Eric Fuchs	Geneva	Switzerland
Tullio Goffi	Brescia	Italy
Antonio Hortelano	Rome/Madrid	Italy/Spain
Oto Mádr	Prague	Czechoslovakia
Richard McCormick SJ	Washington, DC	USA
Enda McDonagh	Maynooth	Ireland
Gaspar Mora	Barcelona	Spain
Helen Oppenheimer	Jersey	Channel Islands
Jean Porter	Nashville, TN	USA
Bernard Quelquejeu OP	Paris	France
Peter Rottländer	Aachen	Germany
José Solozábal	Bilbao	Spain
Marciano Vidal	Madrid	Spain

Members of the Board of Directors

Foundation

A. van den Boogaard	President	Nijmegen	The Netherlands
P. Brand	Secretary	Ankeveen	The Netherlands
M. Palazzi	Treasurer	Doorn	The Netherlands
B. van Iersel		Nijmegen	The Netherlands
J. Coleman		Berkeley, CA	USA
J.-P. Jossua		Paris	France
J.-B. Metz		Münster	Germany

Founders

A. van den Boogaard	Nijmegen	The Netherlands
P. Brand	Ankeveen	The Netherlands
Yves Congar OP	Paris	France
H. Küng	Tübingen	Germany
K. Rahner SJ†	Innsbruck	Austria
E. Schillebeeckx OP	Nijmegen	The Netherlands

Directors/Counsellors

Giuseppe Alberigo	Bologna	Italy
José Oscar Beozzo	São Paolo, SP	Brazil
Willem Beuken SJ	Nijmegen	The Netherlands
Leonardo Boff	Rio de Janeiro	Brazil
Lisa Sowle Cahill	Chestnut Hill, MA	USA
Louis-Marie Chauvet	Paris	France
Julia Ching	Toronto	Canada
John Coleman SJ	Berkeley, CA	USA
M. Shawn Copeland	New Haven, CT	USA
Christian Duquoc OP	Lyons	France
Virgil Elizondo	San Antonio, TX	USA
Elisabeth Schüssler Fiorenza	Cambridge MA	USA
Seán Freyne	Dublin	Ireland
Gustavo Gutiérrez	Lima	Peru
Hermann Häring	Nijmegen	The Netherlands
Bas van Iersel SMM	Nijmegen	The Netherlands
Werner Jeanrond	Lund	Sweden
Jean-Pierre Jossua OP	Paris	France
Maureen Junker-Kenny	Dublin	Ireland
François Kabasele Lumbala	Mbuji Mayi	Zaïre
Karl-Josef Kuschel	Tübingen	Germany
Nicholas Lash	Cambridge	Great Britain
Mary-John Mananzan OSB	Manila	Philippines

Norbert Mette	Münster	Germany
Johann-Baptist Metz	Münster	Germany
Dietmar Mieth	Tübingen	Germany
Jürgen Moltmann	Tübingen	Germany
Mercy Amba Ochuyoye	Princeton	USA
John Panagopoulos	Athens	Greece
Aloysius Pieris SJ	Gonawala-Kelaniya	Sri Lanka
James Provost	Washington, DC	USA
Giuseppe Ruggieri	Catania	Italy
Christoph Theobald SJ	Paris	France
Miklós Tomka	Budapest	Hungary
David Tracy	Chicago, IL	USA
Marciano Vidal CSSR	Madrid	Spain
Knut Walf	Nijmegen	The Netherlands

General Secretariat: Prins Bernardstraat 2, 6521 AB Nijmegen, the Netherlands
Manager: Mrs E.C. Duindam-Deckers.

Some Back Issues of *Concilium* still available

All listed issues published before 1991 are available at £6.95 each. Issues published after 1991 are £8.95 each. Add 10% of value for postage.
US, Canadian and Philippian subscribers contact: Orbis Books, Shipping Dept., Maryknoll, NY 10545 USA
Special rates are sometimes available for large orders. Please write for details.

1974

91	The Church as Institution: *Sociological studies*
92	Politics and Liturgy: *Eucharist, liberation, etc.*
93	Jesus Christ & Human Freedom: *Lash, Schillebeeckx, Gutiérrez*
100	Sexuality in Catholicism: *History, sociology, dogma, education*

1978/1979

113	Revelation & Experience *Definitions, language, individualism*
116	Buddhism and Christianity *Suffering, liberation, reports*
118	An Ecumenical Confession of Faith: *Anglican, Orthodox, etc.*
121	The Family in Crisis or in Transition: *Theology and social science*

1980

133	Right of Community to a Priest: *Statistics, biography, theology*
134	Women in a Man's Church: *History, the present, theology*
137	Electing our own Bishops: *History, theology, organization*
139	Christian Obedience: *Boff, Schillebeeckx, Duquoc*

1981

141	Neo-conservatism: *A worldwide survey*
142	Times of Celebration: *Church, family and community*
143	God as Father?: *Congar, Moltmann, Sölle, Ruether, C. Halkes*
144	Tension between the Churches: *Elizondo, Greinacher*
145	Nietzsche and Christianity: *Relevance, challenge, value*
146	Where does the Church Stand?: *New developments, Vatican II etc.*
147	The Revised Code of Canon Law: *Expectations, Code, Reactions*
148	Who has the Say in the Church?: *Ecumenical debate of Magisteri*
150	Christian Ethics: *Uniformity, Pluralism*

1982

151	The Church and Racism: *Theory, doctrine and local reports*
154	Churches in E. European Socialist Societies: *Historical surveys*
155	Being Human a Criterion of Being Christian: *Schillebeeckx*
158	Right to Dissent: *R.E. Murphy, Miguez Bonino: biblical norms*

1983

- 166 Cosmology and Theology: *The NT and today, H.Chadwick, M.Hesse*
- 167 The Ecumenical Council: *History, laws, today*
- 169 Job and the Silence of God: *From Bible to today, Westermann*
- 170 Twenty Years of Concilium: *Schillebeeckx, Küng, Rahner, Congar*

1984

- 171 Different Theologies: *Gutiérrez, Schussler Fiorenza, Kasemann*
- 172 Ethics of Liberation: *Liberation of ethics worldwide*
- 173 The Sexual Revolution: *Situation problems, Christian reaction*
- 174 Transmitting Faith to Next Generation: *What, how, to whom?*
- 175 The Holocaust as Interruption: *Articles by Jews and Christians*
- 176 La Iglesia popular: *Gutiérrez, Boff, Schillebeeckx*
- 177 Monotheism: *History, theology, today: Moltmann, Vahanian, Dumas*
- 179 Suicide and the Right to Die: *Ethical and theological issues*
- 180 The Teaching Authority of Believers: *Bible, case histories*

1985-7

- 182 Woman Invisible in Church & Theology: *Structures, case studies*
- 183 Christianity among World Religions: *Islam, Hinduism, Buddhism*
- 184 Forgiveness: *Anthropology, theology, spirituality*
- 185 Canon Law: *Practical implications of the new code*
- 186 Popular Religion: *Examples, theology, implications*
- 187 The Option for the Poor: *Reality, tradition, challenges*
- 188 Synod 1985: *Preparation, the meeting, the results*
- 189 The Exodus Paradigm: *Bible, tradition, hermeneutics, today*
- 190 The Fate of Confession: *Tradition, problems, pastoral issues*
- 191 Changing Values and Virtues: *Social facts, reflection*
- 192 Orthodoxy and Heterodoxy: *History, theology, practice*
- 193 The Church and Christian Democracy: *Case Studies*
- 194 Woman, Work, Poverty: *Analyses, case studies, reflections*

1988

- 195 A Council for Peace: *Moltmann, Sobrino, Küng*
- 196 Christian Identity: *From the inside and the outside*
- 197 Power in the Church: *History and institution, S. Sykes on C of E*
- 198 Diakonia: Church for Others: *Needs and conflicts in service*
- 199 Theologies of the Third World: *Boff, Balasuriya, James Cone*

1989

- 201 The French Revolution: *Church reactions then and subsequently*
- 202 Music and the Experience of God: *Liturgy, Black Africa,*
- 203 Ethics in the Natural Sciences: *General and specific issues*
- 204 World Catechism: *Unity and diversity in the churches*
- 205 Sport: *Social role, culture, ethics*
- 206 Motherhood experience: *Institution, Theology*

1990

- 1990/1 On the Threshold of the Third Millennium: *Congress issue edited by Concilium Foundation*
- 1990/2 The Ethics of World Religions and Human Rights: *Küng and Moltmann*
- 1990/3 Asking and Thanking: *Duquoc and Floristán*
- 1990/4 Collegiality put to the Test: *Provost and Walf*
- 1990/5 Coping with Failure: *Greinacher and Mette*
- 1990/6 1492-1992 The Voice of the Victims: *Boff and Elizondo*

1991

- 1991/1 The Bible and Its Readers: *Beuken, Freyne and Weiler*
- 1991/2 The Pastoral Care of the Sick: *Collins and Power*
- 1991/3 Aging: *Sowle Cahill and Mieth*
- 1991/4 No Heaven without Earth: *Metz and Schillebeeckx*
- 1991/5 *Rerum Novarum*: One Hundred Years of Catholic Social Teaching *Baum and Coleman*
- 1991/6 The Special Nature of Women?: *Carr and Schüssler Fiorenza*

1992

- 1992/1 Towards the African Synod: *Alberigo and Ngindu Mashete*
- 1992/2 The New Europe: *Greinacher and Mette*
- 1992/3 Fundamentalism as an Ecumenical Challenge: *Küng and Moltmann*
- 1992/4 Where is God? A Cry of Human Distress: *Duquoc and Floristán*
- 1992/5 The Tabu of Democracy within the Church: *Provost and Walf*
- 1992/6 The Debate on Modernity: *Geffre and Jossua*

1993

- 1993/1 Messianism through History: *Beuken and Weiler*
- 1993/2 Any Room for Christ in Asia?: *Boff and Elizondo in collaboration with Pieris and Mananzan*
- 1993/3 The Spectre of Mass Death: *Power and Lumbala*
- 1993/4 Migrants and Refugees: *Mieth and Cahill*
- 1993/5 Reincarnation or Resurrection?: *Häring and Metz*
- 1993/6 Mass Media: *Coleman and Tomka*

1994

- 1994/1 Violence against Women: *Schüssler Fiorenza and Copeland*
- 1994/2 Christianity and Cultures: A Mutual Enrichment: *Greinacher and Mette*
- 1994/3 Islam: A Challenge for Christianity: *Küng and Moltmann*
- 1994/4 Mysticism and the Institutional Crisis: *Duquoc and Gutiérrez*
- 1994/5 Catholic Identity: *Provost and Walf*
- 1994/6 Why Theology?: *Jeanrond and Jeffré*

Please send orders and remittances to:
SCM Press Ltd, 26-30 Tottenham Road, London N1 4BZ

Two Exciting Journals - Now Available from Orbis Books

Studies in World Christianity
Editor: James P. Mackay, Edinburgh University

This brand new journal gives visible expression to currents set in motion by the Center for the Study of Christianity in the Non-Western World at Edinburgh University. Reporting on developments in world religious studies, theology, and the science of religion, **Studies in World Christianity** will make available for the first time valuable insights on the re-emergence of religious traditions and cultures worldwide.

International Advisory Board includes Elsa Tamez, Chen Ze Min, Gnana Robinson, David Tracy, Charles Forman, Paul Swanson, Mary-John Manazan, Kwame Bediako, Gregory Baum, Joon Surh Park, Chun Chae Ok, Gary Trompf, Michael Pye, Jyotsna Chatterfi, David Turner, Geza Vermes.

Studies in Interreligious Dialogue
Lead Editor: Henk Vroom, Free University, Amsterdam

Since 1991, **Studies in Interreligious Dialogue** has presented articles of high academic quality on the issues and challenges raised in encounters between religious traditions and world views. It promotes discussion on the realities of a pluralistic age while providing points of view of multinational scholars from many religious confessions.

Current Editorial Board includes Muhammed Arkoun, Julia Ching, Diana Eck, Ursula King, Hans Waldenfels, Keith Ward, Felix Wilfred.

PUBLISHED TWICE ANNUALLY, MAY AND OCTOBER.

Studies in World Christianity – $30 - Individuals /$50 - Institutions
Studies in Interreligious Dialogue – $30 - Individuals /$50 - Institutions

EXAMINE EITHER OR BOTH OF THESE JOURNALS FREE FOR 30 DAYS

Just complete and mail this coupon; your single issue will be shipped with a bill payable in 30 days. To continue your subscription, simply remit your check or MC/VISA information. To cancel, just return the issue and invoice.

[ ] **Studies in World Christianity**   [ ] **Studies in Interreligious Dialogue**

Name . . . .
Address . . . .
City/State/ZIP . . . .
Telephone (daytime) . . . .

ORBIS BOOKS, Dept. NJR, Box 308, Maryknoll, NY 10545-0308

Concilium Subscription Information - outside North America

Individual Annual Subscription (six issues): £30.00
Institution Annual Subscription (six issues): £40.00
Airmail subscriptions: add £10.00
Individual issues: £8.95 each

New subscribers please return this form:
for a two-year subscription, double the appropriate rate

(for individuals)   £30.00   (1/2 years)   . . . .

(for institutions)   £40.00   (1/2 years)   . . . .

Airmail postage
outside Europe +£10.00   (1/2 years)   . . . .

                                        Total . . . .

I wish to subscribe for one/two years as an individual/institution
(delete as appropriate)

Name/Institution . . . .

Address . . . .

. . . .

. . . .

I enclose a cheque for . . . . payable to SCM Press Ltd

Please charge my Access/Visa/Mastercard no. . . . .

Signature . . . . Expiry Date . . . .

Please return this form to:
SCM PRESS LTD 26-30 Tottenham Road, London N1 4BZ

CONCILIUM

The Theological Journal of the 1990s

Now available from Orbis Books

Founded in 1965 and published six times a year, *Concilium* is a world-wide journal of theology. Its editors and essayists encompass a veritable 'who's who' of theological scholars. Not only the greatest names in Catholic theology, but exciting new voices from every part of the world, have written for this unique journal.

Concilium exists to promote theological discussion in the spirit of Vatican II, out of which it was born. It is a catholic journal in the widest sense: rooted firmly in the Catholic heritage, open to other Christian traditions and the world's faiths. Each issue of *Concilium* focusses on a theme of crucial importance and the widest possible concern for our time. With contributions from Asia, Africa, North and South America, and Europe, *Concilium* truly reflects the multiple facets of the world church.

Now available from Orbis Books, *Concilium* will continue to focus theological debate and to challenge scholars and students alike.

Please enter my subscription to **Concilium 1996/1-6**
[ ] individual US$60.00   [ ] institutional US$75.00
[ ] SAVE $20: 2-yr subscription $100 individuals $130 institutions

Please send the following back issues at US$15.00 each

1995 . . . . 1994 . . . .
1993 . . . . 1992 . . . .

[ ] MC/Visa . . . . . . / . . . . . . / . . . . . . / . . . . . Expires . . . .
[ ] Check (payable to Orbis Books)

Name/Institution . . . .

Address . . . .

City/State/Zip . . . .

Telephone . . . .

Send order and payment to:
Orbis Books, Box 302, Maryknoll, NY 10545-0302 USA
Issues subject to availability. Prices subject to change.

www.ingramcontent.com/pod-product-compliance
Lightning Source LLC
Chambersburg PA
CBHW051403290426
44108CB00015B/2135